PEP

Ability Test

Practice Book 2

Sarah Collins, Peter Francis, Andrew Hammond,
David E Hanson, Alison Head, Louise Martine,
Chris Pearce, Alison Primrose

Every effort has been made to trace all copyright holders, but if any have been inadvertently overlooked, the Publishers will be pleased to make the necessary arrangements at the first opportunity.

Although every effort has been made to ensure that website addresses are correct at time of going to press, Hachette Learning cannot be held responsible for the content of any website mentioned in this book. It is sometimes possible to find a relocated web page by typing in the address of the home page for a website in the URL window of your browser.

Hachette UK's policy is to use papers that are natural, renewable and recyclable products and made from wood grown in well-managed forests and other controlled sources. The logging and manufacturing processes are expected to conform to the environmental regulations of the country of origin.

To order, please visit www.hachettelearning.com or contact Customer Service at education@hachette.co.uk / +44 (0)1235 827827.

ISBN: 978 1 3983 8846 8

© Sarah Collins, Peter Francis, Andrew Hammond, David E Hanson, Alison Head, Louise Martine, Chris Pearce, Alison Primrose 2025

First published in 2025 by
Hachette Learning,
An Hachette UK Company
Carmelite House
50 Victoria Embankment
London EC4Y 0DZ
www.hachettelearning.com

Impression number   10 9 8 7 6 5 4 3 2 1
Year   2027 2026 2025

The authorised representative in the EEA is Hachette Ireland, 8 Castlecourt Centre, Dublin 15, D15 XTP3, Ireland (email: info@hbgi.ie).

All rights reserved. Apart from any use permitted under UK copyright law, no part of this publication may be reproduced or transmitted in any form or by any means, electronic or mechanical, including photocopying and recording, or held within any information storage and retrieval system, without permission in writing from the publisher or under licence from the Copyright Licensing Agency Limited. Further details of such licences (for reprographic reproduction) may be obtained from the Copyright Licensing Agency Limited, www.cla.co.uk.

Cover illustration by Heather Clarke, D'Avila Illustration Agency

Illustrations by Vian Oelofsen and Stéphan Theron

Typeset in FS Albert 15 on 17pt by IO Publishing

Printed in the UK by Bell and Bain Ltd, Glasgow

A catalogue record for this title is available from the British Library.

Contents

Sections

Section 1 Word analogies 5
Section 2 Spot the difference 8
Section 3 Choose a word to fit the space 12
Section 4 Statement logic 16
Section 5 Essential part 22
Section 6 Words in a sequence 25
Section 7 Number sequences 30
Section 8 Number analogies 36

Maths workouts

Maths workout 1 41
Maths workout 2 44
Maths workout 3 46
Maths workout 4 48
Maths workout 5 51
Maths workout 6 53
Maths workout 7 55

Practice papers

About the practice papers 58
Practice paper 1 59
Practice paper 2 72
Practice paper 3 86
Practice paper 4 100

Exam tips and guidelines 113

Section 1 — Word analogies

Skills notes

- *Word analogy:* to identify the link or connection between words.

  For example:

  Punctual is to late as wise is to …

   A clever

   B bored

   C (foolish)

   D thoughtful

  'Punctual' is to 'late' as 'wise' is to 'foolish' because both pairs are opposites.

Tip

Remember: Look for how words are connected. These connections can include:

- Synonyms – words with similar meanings (e.g. *big* and *large*)
- Antonyms – words with opposite meanings (e.g. *light* and *dark*)
- Function – how things are used (e.g. *broom* is to *sweep* as *pen* is to *write*)
- Part and whole – relationships like *branch* is part of a *tree*
- Sequence – stages or order (e.g. *child* to *adult*)
- Homonyms – words that sound the same or are spelled the same but have different meanings (e.g. *bark* from a dog and *bark* on a tree)

Section 1 Word analogies

Just for fun

Synonyms and antonyms

1. Draw lines to match each word to its synonym.

   mischievous — naughty
   ripple — wrinkle
   naughty — amusing / funny

   (Words on right: wrinkle, amusing, funny)

2. Write the missing letters on the lines provided to complete the word on the right, so that it is an antonym of the word on the left.

   a) hollow   s __ __ i __
   b) beginner   __ __ p e r __
   c) lethargic   a __ t i __ __

3. Put a tick to say whether each word pair is a synonym or an antonym. Explain why in the last column. The first one has been done for you.

Word pair	Synonym	Antonym	Explanation
rigid – flexible		✔	Rigid means something that cannot bend easily, whereas flexible means something that can bend easily without breaking.
probable – unlikely			
impartial – biased			
urge – persuade			

Challenge

Look at the connections between these words:

Part / whole: petal, flower   Sequence: caterpillar, butterfly
Tool / user: hammer, carpenter

Choose one of these relationships and create your own analogy following the pattern.

_____

_____

Word analogies

Worksheet 1

Circle the word or letter that best completes each statement.

1. Tennis is to court as golf is to …. ...../1
   A bunker   B caddy   C course   D ball

2. Shoe is to lace as belt is to …. ...../1
   A band   B trousers   C bag   D buckle

3. Ascend is to up as descend is to …. ...../1
   A stairs   B fall   C down   D lift

4. Grow is to bigger as shrink is to …. ...../1
   A smaller   B child   C light   D tall

5. Strawberry is to red as banana is to …. ...../1
   A yellow   B skin   C split   D fruit

6. A flake is a small part of snow. What is a small part of rain? ...../1
   Snow is to flake as rain is to …………………………….

7. A car travels on a road. What does a train travel on? ...../1
   Car is to road as train is to …………………………….

8. You use a brush to paint. What tool do you use to write in ink? ...../1
   Paint is to brush as ink is to …………………………….

9. A knife goes with a fork. What goes with a cup? ...../1
   Knife is to fork as cup is to …………………………….

10. A frog starts life as a tadpole. What does a butterfly start life as? ...../1
    Frog is to tadpole as butterfly is to …………………………….

Record your score ...../10

Section 2 Spot the difference

Section 2 Spot the difference

Skills notes

- *Spot the difference:* to identify the word that does not belong in the group by finding a pattern.

  For example:

  Three of the words in the list are related to each other in some way. Find the word that is not linked to the others.

  A shred

  B grate

  C grill

  D mince

  Shred, grate and mince are all ways to cut up food. Grill is different because it is a method of cooking food.

Tip

Can't figure out why the answer in the example is 'grill'?

Work out what the other words have in common. The one that doesn't fit the pattern is the odd one out.

8

Spot the difference

Just for fun

Homonyms

Homonyms sound the same but are spelled differently!

Complete the sentences below using one of the words in the table. Each word can only be used once. Not all of the words are used.

hair	might	court	know	scent	by
pour	hare	whole	no	mite	pore
poor	sent	paw	hole	caught	buy

1 He will .... what to do.

2 It .... be possible to have the parcel .... by post.

3 The hounds picked up the .... of the ....

4 The dog .... its .... in the ....

5 He decided to .... the .... set of CDs.

Draw a line through the word that does not fit into the sentence.

6 One of the costumes had a large white **rough / ruff**.

7 The **choir / quire** sang magnificently.

8 The smell of **thyme / time** filled the air as they walked in the garden.

9 They heard a **peal / peel** of laughter coming across the hall.

10 It was **sow / so** good to get out into the garden.

11 It **would / wood** have **bean / been** quicker to cut **threw / through** the **would / wood**.

12 They were **right / write**. The **pour / poor weather / whether** affected the success of the fete.

Section 2 Spot the difference

Draw a line to match each word on the left with the correct meaning on the right.

13 groan Water falling from the sky

14 hire Become bigger or older

15 reign A flow of water or electricity

16 currant To give someone a job

17 higher A low sound made when upset

18 grown The time a king or queen rules

19 current Greater in height or position

20 rain A small, dried fruit, like a raisin

Write a homonym for each word. State whether the homonym is a noun, a verb or an adjective. (Your word may be more than one.)

21 soar ....

22 bury ....

23 wait ....

24 stake ....

25 blew ....

Challenge

Write a riddle to describe one of the homonyms above.

_____

_____

_____

Worksheet 2

Fill in the blanks using the word banks to help you.

(colonise) (inhabit) (land)

1 Settle, ... and .... are all actions that describe people moving to and living in a place. The odd one out is ..../1

(lamp) (night) (candle)

2 Torch, ... and .... are all objects that produce light. The odd one out is ..../1

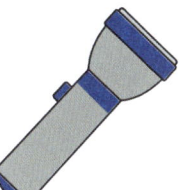   

Which word does not belong?

3 **square, brick, block, cube** ..../1

   Explain your choice: ..../1

Which word is the odd one out?

4 **fur, fleece, feathers, claws** ..../1

   Explain your choice: ..../1

Circle the word that does not belong in the group.

5 A mystery   B query   C puzzle   D enigma   ....../1
6 A previous   B contemporary   C prior   D preceding   ....../1
7 A brilliant B bright   C dazzling   D clever   ....../1
8 A pen   B book   C crayon   D pencil   ....../1

Record your score ....../10

Section 3 Choose a word to fit the space

Skills notes

- *Choose a word to fit the space:* to find the word that makes the sentence complete and logical.

For example:

Select the words that complete the sentence.

Theme parks are a *popular* place for *families* to visit.

A popular; family's

B popularly; family's

C (popular; families)

D popularly; families

'Popular' is an adjective that describes a noun. A place is a noun. 'Families' is the plural of family.

Tip

Remember to look at the grammar and meaning of the sentence to find the best fit.

Choose a word to fit the space

Just for fun

Matching sequences

Look at each of the sequences and circle the one that matches exactly.

Challenge

See if you can solve this extra sequence!

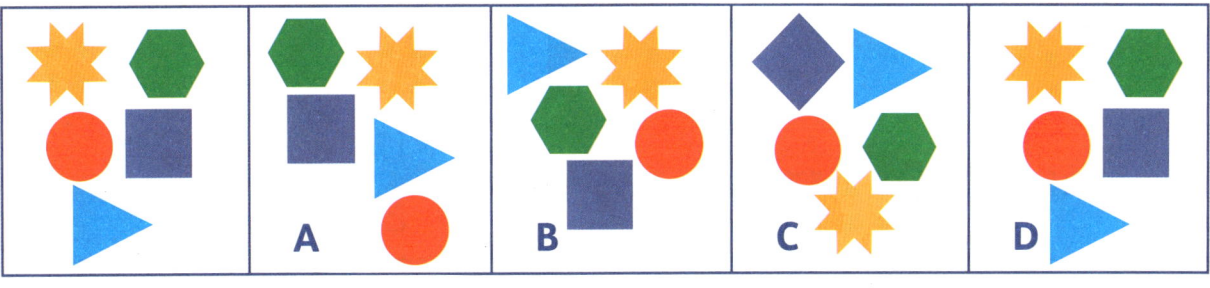

Section 3 Choose a word to fit the space

Worksheet 3

Select the most appropriate pair of words to complete the sentence.

1 The motor vehicle fitness … will definitely … at the end of the month. ...../2

    A license; expire   B licence; respire

    C license; respire   D licence; expire

2 It was … to have to wait in the long … . ...../2

    A frustrating; cue   B frustrating; queue

    C frustrated; cue   D frustrated; queue

3 My granddad is a … supporter of the … football team. ...../2

    A fervent; local   B reverent; local

    C fervent; vocal   D reverent; vocal

4 The … set off at a rapid pace and found the … challenging. ...../2

    A cyclist's; ascent   B cyclist's; assent

    C cyclists; ascent   D cyclists; assent

5 The delivery driver was struggling to deliver a … parcel to my … house. ...../2

    A heavy; neighbours   B heavily; neighbours'

    C heavy; neighbour's   D heavily; neighbour's

Choose a word to fit the space

Circle the incorrect word and write the correct sentence underneath.

6 A strong magic portion was brewing in the witch's cauldron. ...../2

Correct sentence: ....

....

7 The delighted audience broke into spontaneous applaud when the actress came on stage. ...../2

Correct sentence: ....

....

8 It sounds like these horses plan to neigh the hole way home. ...../2

Correct sentence: ....

....

9 At the start of the lesson, the students got out they're textbooks. ...../2

Correct sentence: ....

....

10 The teacher taut her class outside in the sunshine. ...../2

Correct sentence: ....

....

Record your score ...../20

Section 4   Statement logic

Skills notes

- *Statement logic:* to identify the statement that must be true based on the facts provided.

For example:

James, Maria and Aayla enjoy visiting the cinema.

James and Aayla always eat popcorn when they watch a movie.

Aayla sometimes enjoys lemonade with her popcorn.

If the above statements are true, this must mean that only one of the following statements can be true. Which one?

A   James and Maria have watched exactly the same movies.

B   Maria never eats popcorn while watching a movie.

C   James sometimes arrives late at the cinema.

D   Aayla always eats popcorn while watching a movie.

The only statement we know is true is that James and Alaya always eat popcorn when they watch a movie.

Tip

Read the options carefully and cross out any that could be false.

Statement logic

> **Just for fun**
>
> **Deductive questions with maps**
>
> Look at this map of a town and use it to write your own deduction question about where one place is in relation to the other places.
>
>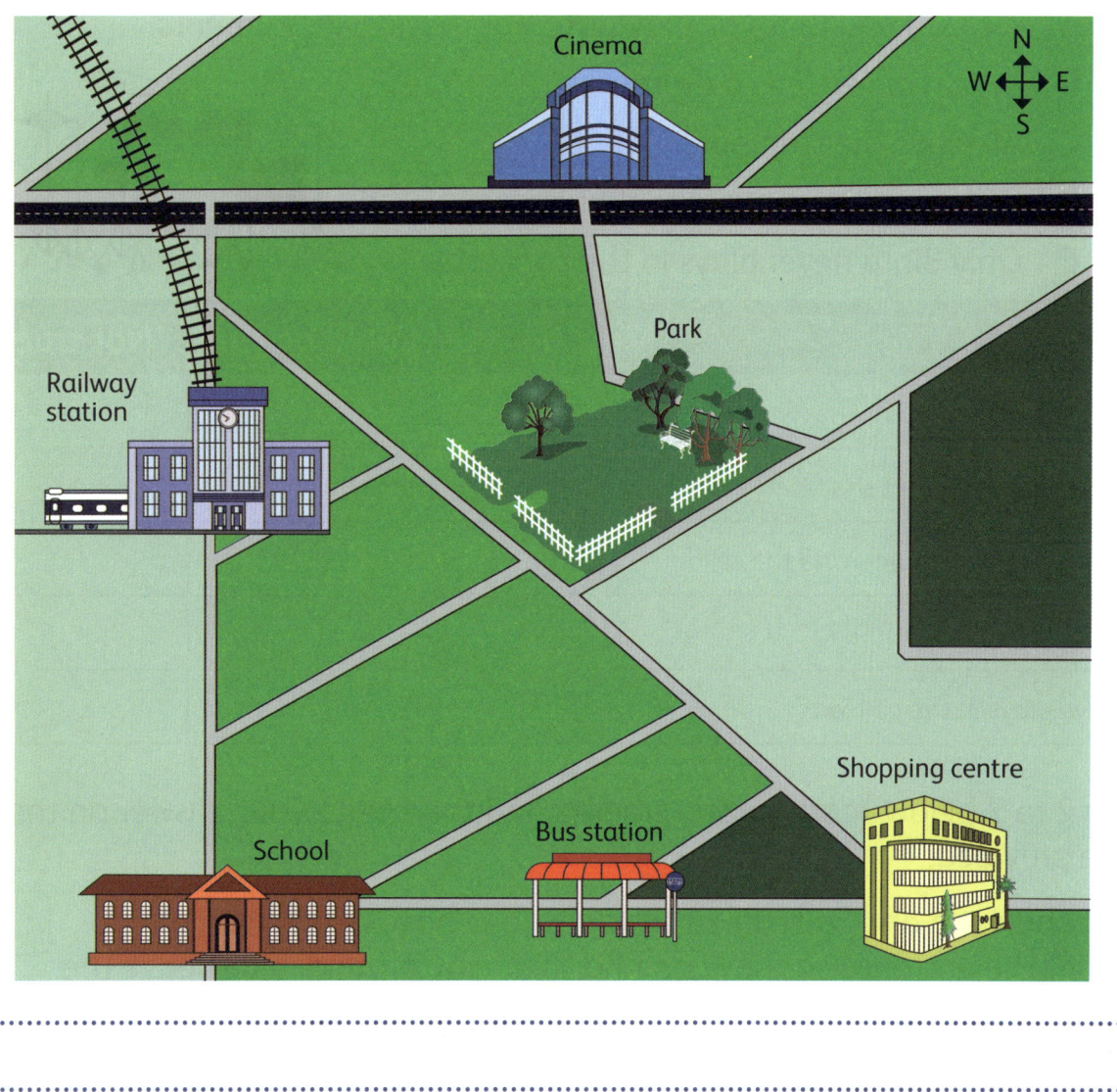
>
> ....
> ....
> ....
> ....

> **Challenge**
>
> Think of a brand-new building that you would like to add to your map. Don't tell your partner what it is but give them a series of deduction clues to see if they can guess correctly.

Section 4 Statement logic

Worksheet 4

Read the instructions for each item carefully.

1 Read the statements below, then check them carefully against the information in the table and complete the table. ...../5

   A Ali, Carl and Binta all play different musical instruments.
   B Every concert has a drummer.
   C Ali plays the trumpet.
   D Binta and Dave play the drums.
   E Only Binta never plays in the concerts.

	Must be true	Could be true	Not true
Carl plays the flute.			
Ali plays in the concerts.			
Binta plays the drums and the cello.			
Ali and Carl are brothers.			
Dave plays in the concerts.			

For 2 to 7 below, read the statements and then write your answer on the line provided.

2 Abi, Katie and Sam are at the zoo. They have been given a map at the entrance so they can find their way around. They leave the entrance and head due west to see the pandas at the end of Marine Walk. Then Sam spots the big cats on the map, so they then head south-east to find them. After two hours of exploring, they decide to have lunch in the café, due north of the entrance. Katie remembers that she has left her gloves on the viewing platform above the elephant enclosure, due south of the pandas. ...../1

What direction must the children head in to collect Katie's gloves?

....

Statement logic

3 Six students took part in a 5 km run. A, B, C, D, E and F all finished in a different order. C did not finish last or first. E overtook A on the finish line. A and B did not come in the first two but were consecutive. F enjoyed the race but tired at the end, finishing after C. D came second.

Who won the race? ....

4 A family of six all sit around a rectangular table. There are four siblings and their parents. Sally and Jane, who are sisters, are next to each other. Harry and James are separated by Gavin, the dad. Jane is not next to her mother Mary. Gavin and Jane are opposite each other. James sits at one end of the table.

Who is sitting opposite James? ....

5 On a go-kart track, six differently coloured cars all entered a tournament. The green car was very fast and did not come last. The race was not won by the red or yellow go-kart but they both defeated the purple go-kart. The blue go-kart came third. The red go-kart came ahead of the yellow go-kart but not next to each other. The pink go-kart came after the purple car.

Who won the race? ....

6 At a college, all students speak English. Of the 40% who speak two languages, French is the second language for half of them. Of the 24% of students who speak three languages, the third that speaks French also speaks Spanish. One-third speaks English, Spanish and Italian. No one else speaks Spanish.

How many more students, as a percentage, speak French than Spanish? ....

7 A van with one driver can make 50 deliveries a day. A company has four vans going out seven days a week. It has six drivers who all work five days a week. On the days when there is an extra driver, the van with two drivers has to make 60 deliveries.

What is the total number of deliveries per week?

....

Section 4 Statement logic

8 K is the fastest front crawl swimmer. L is faster than M at backstroke. M is the slowest at breaststroke. L's favourite stroke is backstroke.

Which of these statements cannot be true? (There is insufficient information to know that any of the statements are definitely true.)

A K is fastest at backstroke.

B M is faster than L at breaststroke.

C M's favourite stroke is backstroke.

D L's fastest stroke is breaststroke.

9 Four friends go shopping. R spends $2 000 at the shops. S spends $500 more than K, and $300 less than R. P spends $500 less than S. Which one of these statements cannot be true?

A S spends $200.

B K spends more than P.

C R spends the most.

D K spends less than R.

10 A shop selling scarves recorded this information: More silk scarves are sold than cotton scarves and twice as many wool scarves are sold as cotton. Pink is the most popular colour of silk scarves. More blue wool scarves are sold than blue silk scarves. The most popular wool scarves are red.

If the above statements are true, this must mean that only one of the following statements can be true. Which one? Circle the letter next to the one true statement.

A Pink silk is more popular than blue wool.

B Blue wool is less popular than red wool.

C Blue silk is more popular than green wool.

D Twice as many pink silk scarves as blue silk scarves are sold.

Statement logic

11 Ben lives at the end of a row of four houses. The red house is between the green house and the orange house. Mary lives in the orange house. Tom lives between Mary and Jane.

If the above statements are true, this must mean that only one of the following statements can be true. Which one? Circle the letter next to the one true statement.

A Ben lives in a blue house.

B Ben lives next to Mary.

C Jane lives in the green house.

D The house at the end is blue.

12 Shep is a black and white collie dog. Benji is a three-year-old dog. Spot is a spaniel with four puppies. Benji and Shep are brothers. Spot and Benji live on the same farm.

If the above statements are true, this must mean that only one of the following statements can be true. Which one? Circle the letter next to the one true statement.

A Spot is Shep's mother.

B Benji is brown and white.

C Shep is a sheep dog.

D Benji is a collie.

Record your score ...../16

Section 5　Essential part

Skills notes

- *Essential part:* to identify a component that the given noun or verb cannot function or exist without, not just something it might have.

For example:

Circle the word that is a necessary component of the word in bold.

Car

A　driver's licence

B　radio

C　(engine)

D　headrest

A car needs an engine to run. It doesn't need a driver's licence, a radio or a headset.

Tip

Remember that the essential part is what the noun or verb absolutely needs to exist or function.

Essential part

Just for fun

Most unlike

Look at these sets of pictures. Identify the one that is most unlike the others. Circle the letter under the correct answer.

For example:

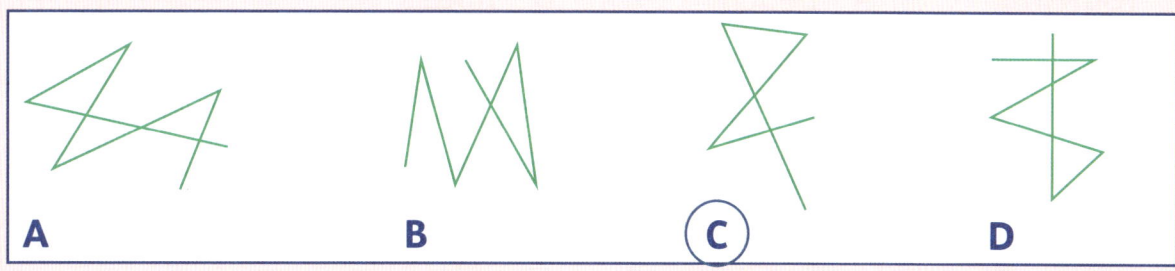

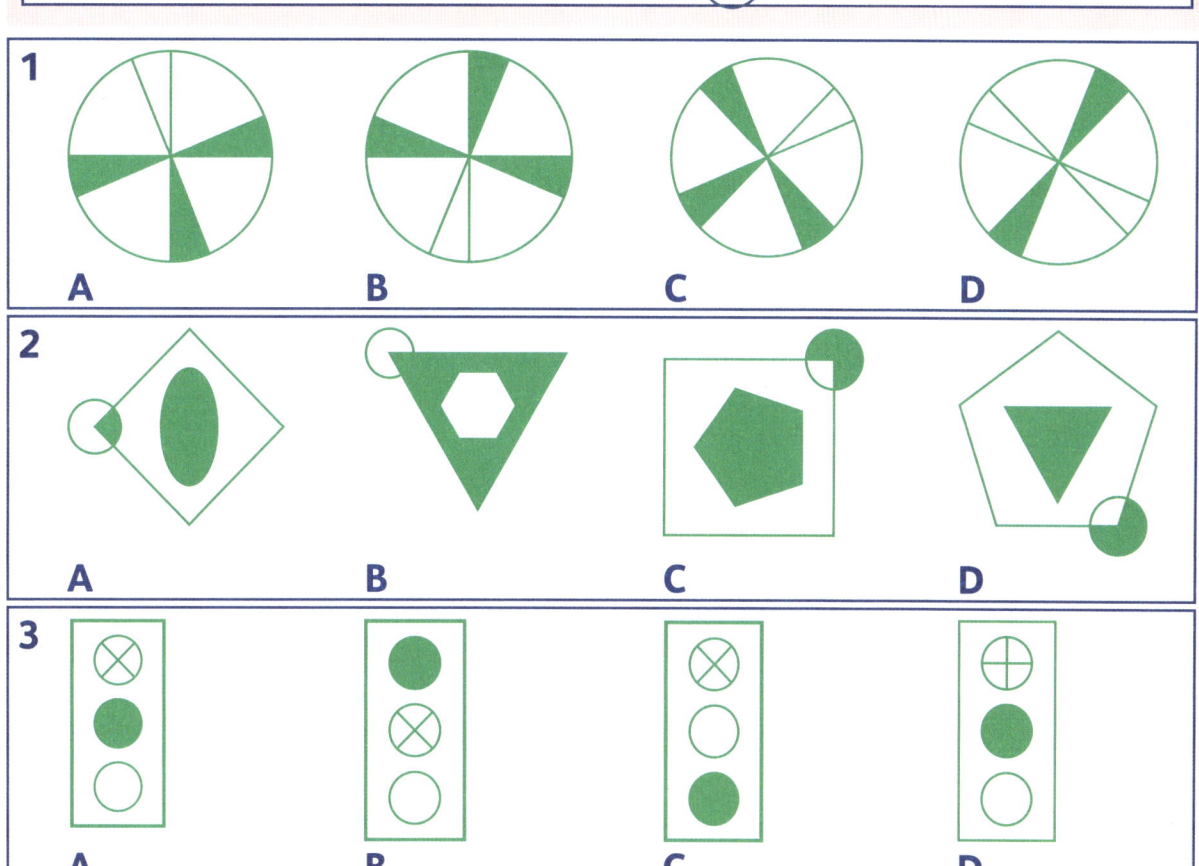

Challenge

Which word is the most unlike the others? Circle your answer and explain your choice.

A jump   B climb   C dance   D mountain

Why? _____

Section 5 Essential part

Worksheet 5

Circle the option that is an essential component of the word in bold.

1 **salary** A money B employment ...../1
 C incentives D bonus

2 **tourism** A beach B hotels ...../1
 C ships D visitors

3 **movie** A theatre B soundtrack ...../1
 C actors D film

4 **pillow** A case B stuffing ...../1
 C sofa D bed

Draw a line through the word that is not an essential component.

5 A zoo wouldn't be a zoo without its **animals / keeper**. ...../1

6 A harbour must be near **a pier / water** to work properly. ...../1

7 The most important thing in a bank is **a camera / money**. ...../1

8 A concert must include tickets. ...../1

 True / False

9 Water is not essential for fish. ...../1

 True / False

10 A choir must have singers. ...../1

 True / False

Record your score ...../10

Section 6 Words in a sequence

Skills notes

- *Word sequence:* to identify the pattern and select the word that comes next.

  For example:

  Select the word that comes next in the sequence.

  inflate, deflate; import, export; include, exclude; immigrate, …

  A immigration

  B (emigrate)

  C immigrated

  D emigrant

  In this pattern, each word is followed by one that means the opposite.

Tip

Always look at how the words change in terms of their spelling, structure or meaning.

Section 6 Words in a sequence

Just for fun

Deductive reasoning

Read the statements and circle the correct answer. You can use the spaces for your workings.

For example:
In four years' time, my grandmother will be exactly five times as old as I am now.

My grandmother is now 56. How old am I?   12

1 The yellow car is 8 km per hour slower than the red car. The blue car is 6 km per hour faster than the yellow car.

   How much faster is the red car than the blue car?

   A 2 km/h **B** 8 km/h **C** 14 km/h **D** 6 km/h

2 Mandy and Annie are twins. Their combined age is one-sixth of their grandmother's age. If their mother is 25 years younger than the grandmother and the twins are now five years old, how old was their mother when Mandy and Annie were born?

   A 25 years old **B** 30 years old **C** 35 years old **D** 40 years old

Words in a sequence

3   In a class of 28 children, 14 attend the football club, ten join the netball club, 12 go to the drama club and ten go to art club. If no one goes to all four clubs, three children attend three clubs, and everyone attends at least one club, how many children attend two clubs?

A 9 **B** 10 **C** 12 **D** 14

Read the statements and answer the questions.

4   There are 34 houses on a paper round. Three houses have two papers every day of the week, ten houses only have a Saturday paper and the rest have five papers a week, one each on Monday, Tuesday, Wednesday, Thursday and Friday. How many papers are delivered on a Monday?

Section 6 Words in a sequence

5 Seven friends have a meal out before going to the theatre. If they spend twice as much on their theatre tickets as at the restaurant, and the total cost for the evening was $168, what was the cost of each theatre ticket?

6 If a tally chart is made of the number of letters that occur in the days of the week, which vowel is the second most frequent?

Challenge

A group of friends went bowling. They paid a total of $14,400 for the evening. Each game costs $600 per person, and they each played three games. How many people were in the group?

Worksheet 6

Circle the word that completes the sequence.

1. associate, association; try, trial; arrive, arrival; refer, … ...../1
   - A referring
   - B referred
   - C preference
   - D referral

2. counterfeit, fake; survey, inspect; modern, current; coarse, … ...../1
   - A course
   - B rough
   - C pleasant
   - D refined

3. despair, hope; expensive, worthless; freedom, captivity; secretive, … ...../1
   - A evasive
   - B surly
   - C frank
   - D serious

4. human, humanly; length, lengthy; beauty, … ...../1
   - A beautiful
   - B beautify
   - C beauties
   - D beautifully

5. bury, burial; depend, dependence; permit, permission; inspect, … ...../1
   - A inspection
   - B inspects
   - C inspected
   - D inspecting

Look at each sequence of word pairs. Fill in the missing word to complete the last pair. ...../5

	Word sequence	Options	Correct word
6	asleep, awake; genuine, real; courteous, unrefined; advance	retreat, fear, ignore, reveal	
7	waste, wastage; wide, width; withdraw, withdrawal; weigh	weight, weighing, weighs, weighing	
8	justice, injustice; humble, proud; serious, trivial; aid	help, hinder, flatter, calm	
9	fracture, break; frosty, cold; do, execute; eager	reluctant, hesitant, joyful, keen	
10	big, huge; anger, enrage; stop, halt; correct	avoid, precise, accurate, false	

Record your score ...../10

Section 7 Number sequences

Skills notes

- *Number sequence:* to identify the pattern in the sequence and find the missing number.

  For example:

  Select the number that completes the sequence.

  7, 14, 21, 28, 35, …

  A 39

  B 42

  C 49

  D 56

  Here, each number increases by 7.

Tip

Look at how the numbers change. Do they increase, decrease or follow a pattern such as doubling?

Number sequences

Just for fun

Apply the code

In each question a given word is written in code. Work out the code and apply it to encode the second word. The alphabet has been provided to help you.

For example:

A B C D E F G H I J K L M N O P Q R S T U V W X Y Z

If the code for READ is PCYB, what is the code for SENT?   QCLR

Encode these words by replacing each letter with the letter that comes next in the alphabet.

A B C D E F G H I J K L M N O P Q R S T U V W X Y Z

1 HORSE ....

2 PAINTER ....

These words have been encoded using the same code. Decode them and write the word.

3 QBODBLF ....

4 WPMDBOP ....

In the next set of questions you are given a word and the same word in code. Describe the code that has been used.

A B C D E F G H I J K L M N O P Q R S T U V W X Y Z

5 TEACH in code is R C Y A F. What is the code?

   ....

6 PRESIDE in code is S U H V L G H. What is the code?

   ....

7 MINUTE in code is I E J Q P A. What is the code?

   ....

Section 7 Number sequences

Now you need to circle the word that is encoded.

A B C D E F G H I J K L M N O P Q R S T U V W X Y Z

8 Is G N Q R D the code for HOUSE or for HORSE?

9 Is Z O X K F X I the code for CRANIAL or CRANIUM?

Here, you must circle the code for the word on the left.

10 PLANTER   TPERXVI

TEMRXIV

TPERXIV

11 CLOAK   AJMYI

AJYMI

AKMYI

Challenge

Complete the table below.

Original word	Code	Rule used	Use the rule to encode the word PARK
DOG	5 16 8	Position +1	
SUN	18 20 13	Position −1	
NOTE	16 17 22 7	Position +2	
CAT	24 2 19	Reverse alphabet position (Z = 1)	

Number sequences

Worksheet 7a

What calculation must be performed on each number in the sequence to produce the next number in the sequence?

1 22 25 28 31 34 ..../1

2 85 77 69 61 53 ..../1

3 64 59 57 52 50 ..../1

4 1 2 4 8 16 32 ..../1

If each number is double the previous number in the sequence plus 2, give the next two numbers in these sequences:

5 6 ..../2

6 3.5 ..../2

Sometimes, the numbers in a sequence don't increase or decrease by the same amount each time. This means the difference isn't constant. To help solve more challenging sequences, we can use two steps:
Step 1: Find the difference between each number in the sequence. Write these differences on the 'Level 1 differences' line.
Step 2: Now look at the pattern you found in Level 1. Work out the differences between those *differences*. Write these on the 'Level 2 differences' line.

7 Sequence: 14   16   19   23   ...../2
   Level 1 differences: +2   +3   ....
   Level 2 differences: +1

8 Sequence: 85   80   74   67   ...../2
   Level 1 differences: −5   −6   ....
   Level 2 differences: −1

Section 7 Number sequences

In these sequences there are two patterns, giving alternate numbers. Identify both patterns and fill in the missing numbers.

9 14   21   15   20   16   19   17   ..../1

10 48   5   47   7   46   9   45   ..../1

Find the next two numbers in these sequences. Working out differences may help.

11 10   17   13   20   16   ..../2

12 6   5   9   8   12   11   ..../2

13 480   240   120   ..../2

14 2   3   5   8   13   ..../2

Record your score ....../22

Number sequences

Worksheet 7b

Select the number that completes the sequence.

1 61, 54, 47, 40, … ...../1
   A 37   B 36   C 33   D 28

2 17, 20, 26, 35, 47, … ...../1
   A 56   B 62   C 68   D 70

3 The next number in this pattern is 28: 31, 33, 30, 32, 29 ..../1
Circle **true** or **false**.

4 The next number in this pattern is 18: 13.5, 15, 16.5 ..../1
Circle **true** or **false**.

5 1, 3, 7, 15, 31, 75 ...../1
Something is wrong in this pattern.
What should the last number be? ....

6 154, 82, 46, 28, 20 ...../1
Something is wrong in this pattern.
What should the last number be? ....

7 Candice is building a pyramid using cube-shaped blocks. ...../1
She starts with 125 blocks on the bottom layer, then uses
64 blocks for the next layer. The layer above that is missing.
Then come layers with 8 blocks and 1 block. How many blocks
should be in the missing layer to keep the pattern going? ....

8 Kyle is stacking books in a pattern. On the first shelf, he ...../1
places 23 books. On the next shelf, he places 17, then 12, then 8.
If the pattern continues, how many books will Kyle place on
the next shelf? ....

9 9, 4, 14, 9, 19, 14, … ...../1
   A 24   B 25   C 27   D 31

10 4, 6, 3, 5, 2, 4, … ...../1
   A 13   B 15   C 1   D 20

Record your score ...../10

Section 8 Number analogies

Skills notes

- *Number analogy:* to find the missing number by identifying a rule and applying it.

For example:

The first two pairs of numbers are related in the same way. Establish the relationship between these pairs and complete the last pair in the same way.

(7 is to 49)
(8 is to 64)
(6 is to …)

A 60

B 30

C 36

D 24

Each number has been squared or multiplied by itself.

Tip

Look for multiplication, addition, subtraction or division patterns between number pairs.

Number analogies

Just for fun

Matrices

One of the options on the right completes the pattern in the grid on the left. Circle the letter beneath the correct answer.

For example:

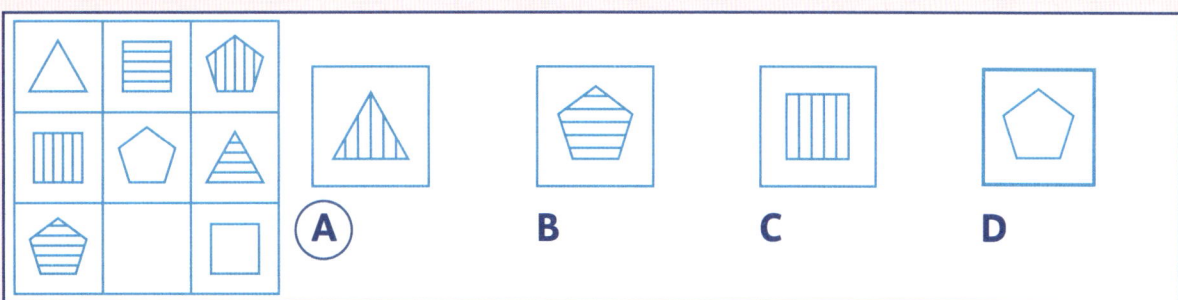

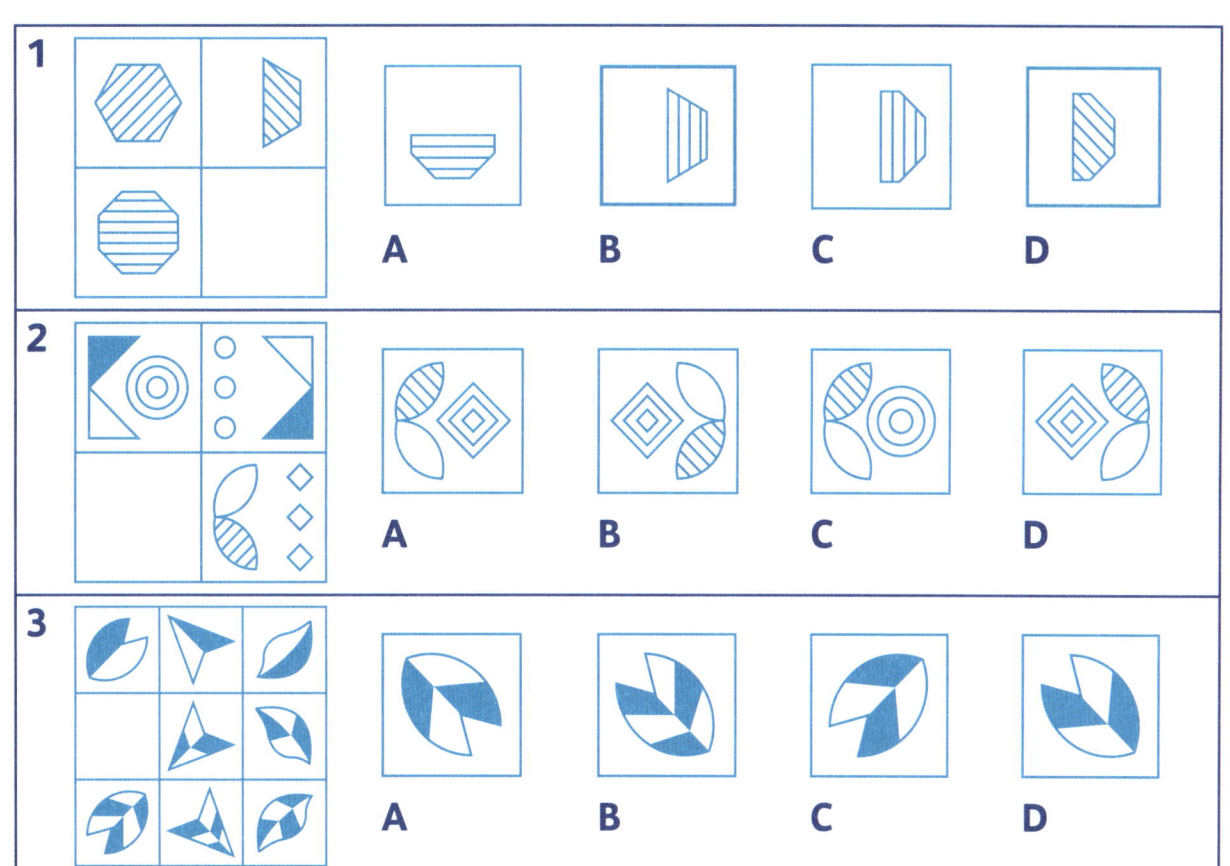

Challenge

Patterns can be in words too. Work out this pattern and complete the final group.

cat, cot, cut   bat, bet, bit   hat, hot, _____

A his   **B** hut   **C** hit   **D** hop

37

Section 8 Number analogies

Worksheet 8a

Begin by practising with just one set of brackets. Work out what has been done with the outer numbers to give the middle number, then decide whether the rule written down is correct or incorrect. Put a ✓ or ✗ next to each rule.

1 (18 [6] 3)   Divide the first number by the third to give the middle number. ..../1

2 (6 [13] 1)   Add the first and third number and multiply the answer by 2 to give the middle number. ..../1

3 (2 [8] 5)   Add 5 to the third number to give the middle number. ..../1

4 (3 [10] 1)   Multiply the first number by itself and add the third number to give the middle number. ..../1

5 (18 [4] 14) Subtract the third number from the first to give the middle number. ..../1

6 (9 [3] 7)   Divide the first number by 2 to give the middle number. ..../1

7 (4 [21] 3)   Add the first and third numbers and multiply by 3 to give the middle number. ..../1

Number analogies

Now see if you can work with two sets of brackets. For each question decide whether the middle number in both pairs has been given using the same rule. Put a ✓ or ✗ next to each one.

8 (4 [10] 6)   (11 [15] 4)   ...../1

....

9 (2 [6] 3)   (15 [18] 3)   ...../1

....

10 (4 [18] 3)   (9 [12] 2)   ...../1

....

11 (12 [16] 20)   (9 [12] 15)   ...../1

....

Can you describe the rule being used? Both sets of brackets in each question follow the same rule.

12 (6 [13] 20)   (4 [11] 18)   ...../1

....

13 (9 [4] 1)   (17 [7] 3)   ...../1

....

14 (4 [24] 3)   (5 [30] 3)   ...../1

....

Record your score ...../14

39

Section 8 Number analogies

Worksheet 8b

The three numbers in each set of brackets in each question are all related in the same way. Work out how they are related from the first two sets of brackets, then apply the same pattern to complete the third set. Write the missing numbers on the lines provided.

1 (3 [18] 6)   (2 [8] 4)   (9 [........] 7)   ...../1

2 (1 [18] 8)   (3 [14] 4)   (5 [........] 6)   ...../1

3 (5 [88] 18)   (2 [42] 22)   (7 [........] 14)   ...../1

4 (9 [3] 3)   (16 [8] 2)   (36 [........] 6)   ...../1

5 (2 [12] 6)   (4 [16] 4)   (5 [........] 12)   ...../1

6 (6 [9] 12)   (8 [12] 16)   (10 [........] 20)   ...../1

7 (9 [17] 10)   (4 [9] 7)   (16 [........] 5)   ...../1

8 (36 [18] 2)   (24 [4] 6)   (12 [........] 3)   ...../1

9 (3 [14] 4)   (6 [24] 6)   (10 [........] 1)   ...../1

10 (3 [13] 2)   (1 [11] 4)   (5 [........] 7)   ...../1

Record your score ...../10

Maths workout 1

Finding the original amount

Write your answers on the lines provided. Use the space below each item for working out.

1 When a number is divided by 3 and this result is multiplied by 8, the final answer is 24.

What was the number? ....

2 When a number is multiplied by 3 and this result is divided by 10, the final answer is 12.

What was the number? ....

3 If $\frac{1}{11}$ of the total amount is 2, what is the total amount?

....

Maths workout 1

4 If $\frac{7}{8}$ of the total amount is 14, what is the total amount?

....

5 If $\frac{5}{6}$ of an amount of money is $350, what is the whole amount?

....

6 When a number is divided by 2, the result is 105. What was the number? ....

Maths workout 1

7 When our father shares out the money in his jar equally among four children, they each get $1 500. How much money was in the jar?

....

8 What is the mass of a full bag of sand, if $\frac{7}{9}$ of the bag has a mass of 4.2 kg? ....

9 A chef uses 45 kg of potatoes. This was $\frac{5}{6}$ of his total supply. What was the mass of his total supply? ....

Maths workout 2

Formulae

Write your answers on the lines provided.

1. a) A car travels at 40 km/h. How long does it take to travel:

   i. 10 km ....

   ii. 80 km? ....

   b) Write a formula for the time it takes the car to travel *n* km at this speed. ....

2. Robert thought of a number. He multiplied it by 7 and then added 6.

   a) Write an expression to represent his final result. ....

   b) If Robert thought of the number 5, what was his final result?

   ....

44

3 Write these word sentences as formulae. Use brackets where appropriate.

a) Subtract a from b and divide the result by 2. ....

....

b) Divide c by d and add e to the result. ....

....

4 Rosie thought of a number. She multiplied it by 2 and then added 5.

a) Write an expression to represent her final result.

....

....

b) If Rosie's final result was 7, what number did she first think of?

....

....

Maths workout 3

Pictograms

Look carefully at the pictograms, then answer the questions.

1. The pictogram below shows the number of marks achieved by a group of learners in a spelling test.

    ■ Marks in a spelling test

Oriel	✓ ✓ ✓ ✓ ✓ ✓ ✓
Sam	✓ ✓ ✓
Chris	✓ ✓ ✓ ✓ ✓
Maya	✓ ✓
Edward	✓ ✓ ✓ ✓

    Key: ✓ represents 1 mark

    a) Who scored the highest mark? **A** Oriel **B** Sam **C** Chris **D** Maya **E** Edward ....

    b) Maya got fewer marks than Sam. Circle **true** or **false**.

    c) What is the difference between the highest and lowest scores?
    ....

    d) How many learners got more than 4 marks out of 8?
    A 1 **B** 2 **C** 3 **D** 4 ....

2. The pictogram below shows the money raised for charity by four friends.

    ■ Money raised for charity

Toby	$ $
Max	$ $ $
Camilla	$ $ $ $
Dorothy	$ $ $ $ $ $
Esther	$ $ $ $ $

    Key: $ represents $500

a) Who raised the most money? ....

b) How much more money did Dorothy raise than Toby? **A** $1 500 **B** $2 000 **C** $2 500 **D** $3 000 ....

c) How much money was raised altogether?

....

d) Two friends raised $5 000 in total. Who were they?

....

3   The chart shows the number of bottles of water sold from the vending machine during one week.

■ Bottles of water sold in one week

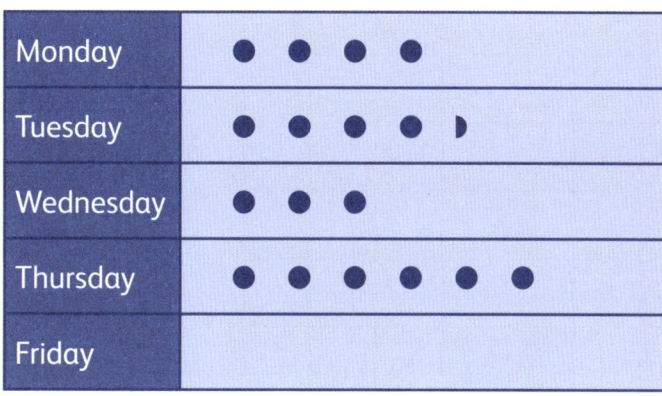 

Key: ● represents four bottles

a) How many bottles of water were sold on Thursday?
   A 20   **B** 22   **C** 24   **D** 28 ....

b) How many bottles of water were sold on Tuesday?

....

c) On Friday, 20 bottles of water were sold. Fill in the results for Friday.

d) What was the total number of bottles sold that week?

....

Maths workout 4

Bar charts

Write your answers on the lines provided.

1. This bar chart shows the number of different types of pets owned by learners in Grade 6.

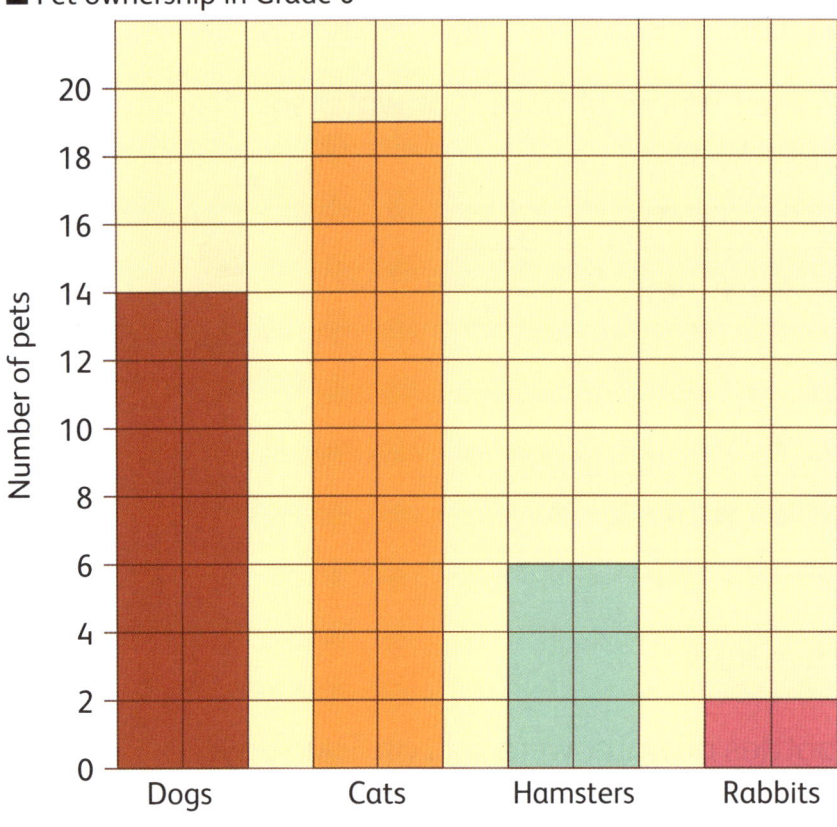

a) How many dogs are owned by learners in Grade 6?

....

b) How many cats are owned by learners in Grade 6?

....

c) How many more cats are owned than rabbits?

....

d) How many pets do Grade 6 learners own in total?

....

2 Archie's cat has had six kittens. The bar chart shows the masses of five of the kittens.

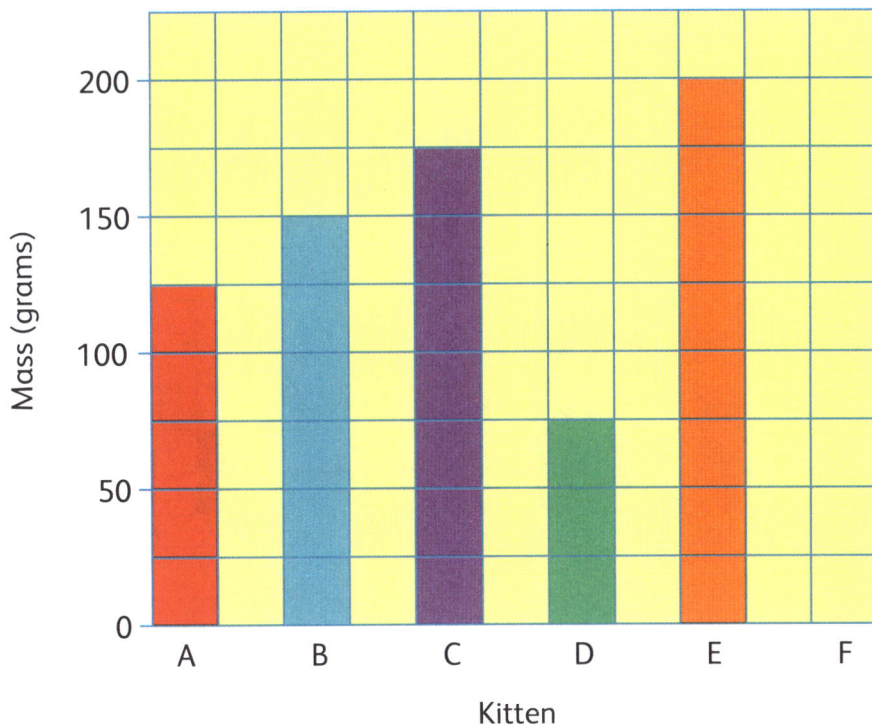

a) What is the mass of kitten C?

....

b) What is the mass of kitten A, in kilograms?

....

c) The total mass of the six kittens is 900 g. Calculate the mass of kitten F, in grams.

....

d) Draw the bar to show the mass of kitten F on the bar chart above.

Maths workout 4

3 The bar chart shows the number of ice creams sold over a one-year period.

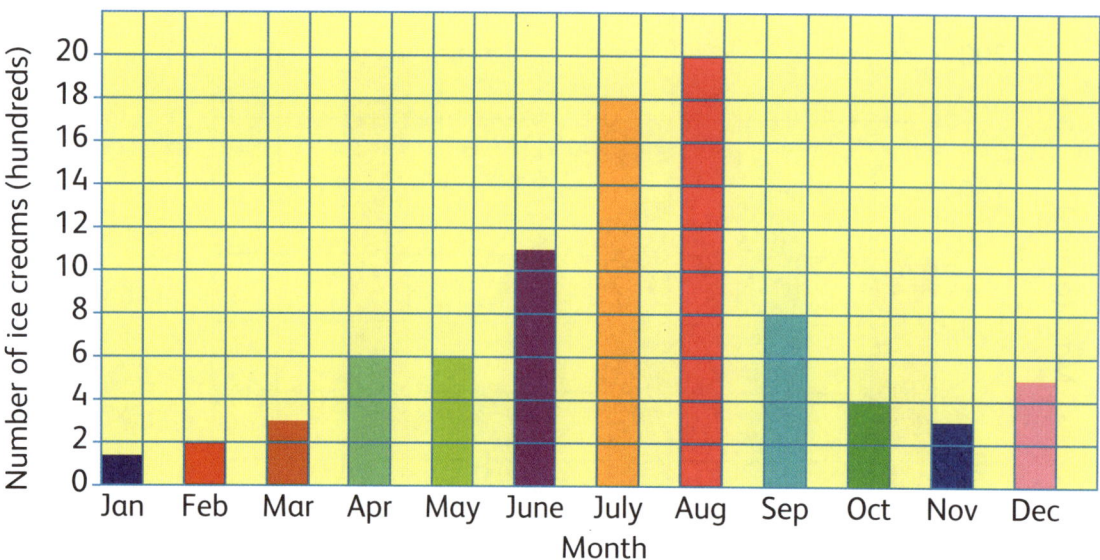

a) Which month had the lowest number of ice cream sales?
   A January   **B** February   **C** December   **D** March

   ....

b) The highest number of ice creams was sold in

   ....

c) i. In which two months were the same number of ice creams sold?

   ....

   ii. How many ice creams were sold altogether during these two months?

   ....

d) The sales of ice creams increase leading up to August. Suggest a reason for this. ....

....

Maths workout 5

Frequency diagrams

Write your answers in the table provided below.

1 The school football team played 15 matches this term. The number of goals they scored in each match are shown below.

1   0   2   3   2   2   4   5
0   1   2   3   0   1   2

Goals scored in a match	Tally	Frequency
0	III	3
1		
2		
3		
4		
5		
	Total	

a) Complete the table for the number of goals scored.

b) Draw a frequency diagram to show the information in the table.

2 This frequency diagram shows the shoe sizes of Grade 6 learners.

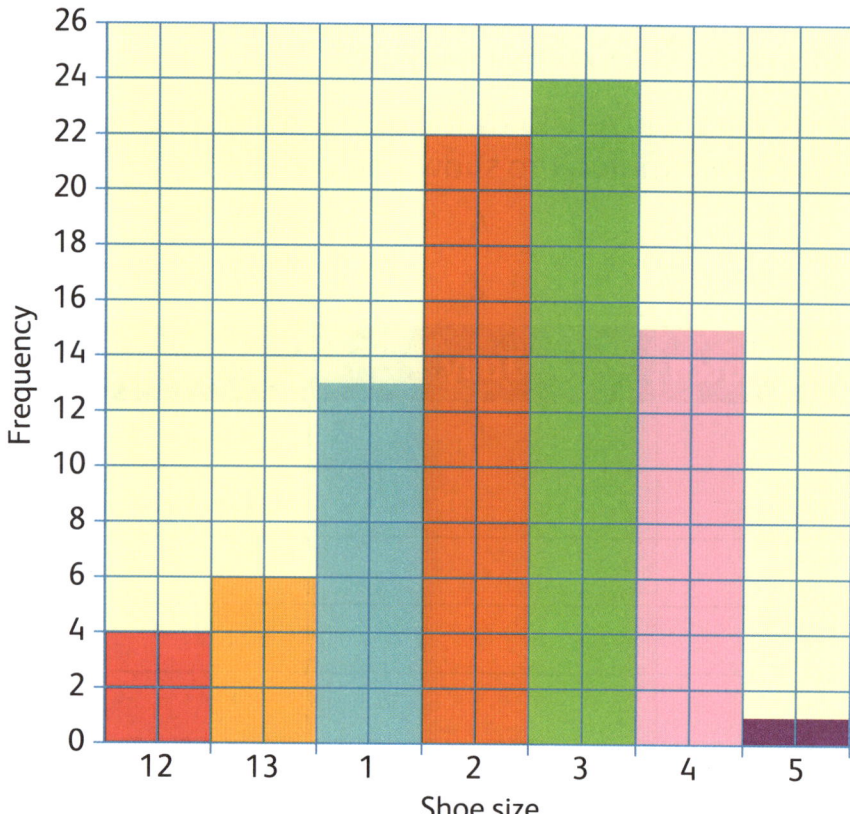

■ Shoe sizes in Grade 6

a) How many learners have shoe size 12 or 13?

   ....

b) How many learners have shoe size 1 or larger?

   ....

c) How many learners are there in the class?

   ....

Maths workout 6

Pie charts

1. This pie chart shows the results of a survey about car ownership.

   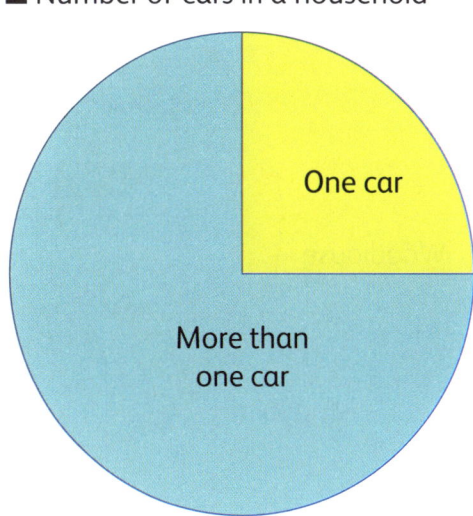
   ■ Number of cars in a household

   a) What fraction of households surveyed have only one car?

   ....

   b) What percentage of households surveyed have only one car?

   ....

   c) What percentage of households surveyed have more than one car?

   ....

   d) The survey was completed by 200 households. How many of the household have only one car?

   ....

2. In the autumn term, learners in Grade 6 choose between playing rugby, soccer, netball or hockey. This pie chart displays the sports chosen by Grade 6 last year.

   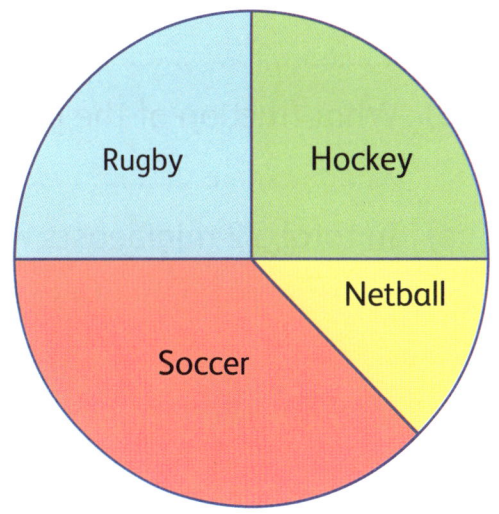
   ■ Sports chosen by learners in Grade 6

   a) What percentage of Grade 6 learners chose rugby? **A** 15% **B** 25% **C** 30% **D** 40%

   ....

   b) The fraction of learners who chose netball was:

   ....

   c) More than half of the learners chose soccer. Circle **true** or **false**.

   d) Twelve learners chose rugby. How many learners were in Grade 6?

   ....

53

Maths workout 6

3 The pie chart shows information about the spiders and insects found on a nature walk.

■ Spiders and insects found on a nature walk

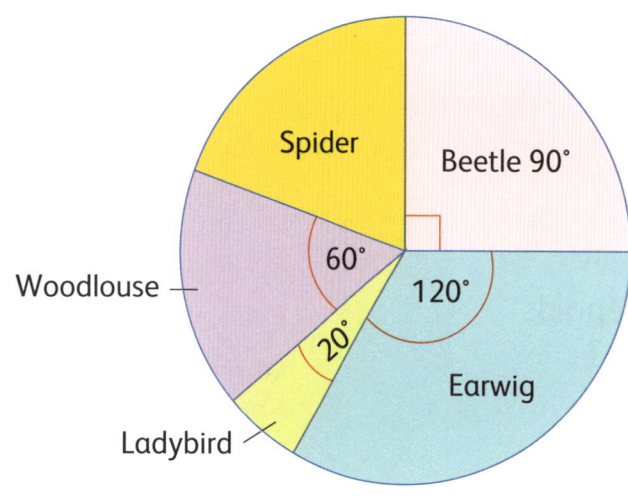

The angle sum at the centre of a circle is 360°

a) What fraction of the pie chart represents beetles?

....

b) What fraction of the pie chart represents earwigs?

....

c) Calculate the size of the angle that represents spiders.

....

d) What fraction of the pie chart represents spiders?

....

e) In total, 72 minibeasts were found.

   i. How many beetles were found?

   ....

   ii. How many earwigs were found?

   ....

   iii. How many ladybirds were found?

   ....

Maths workout 7

Line graphs

1 This line graph shows the amount of fuel in Stanley's car during a car journey.

■ Fuel used during a journey

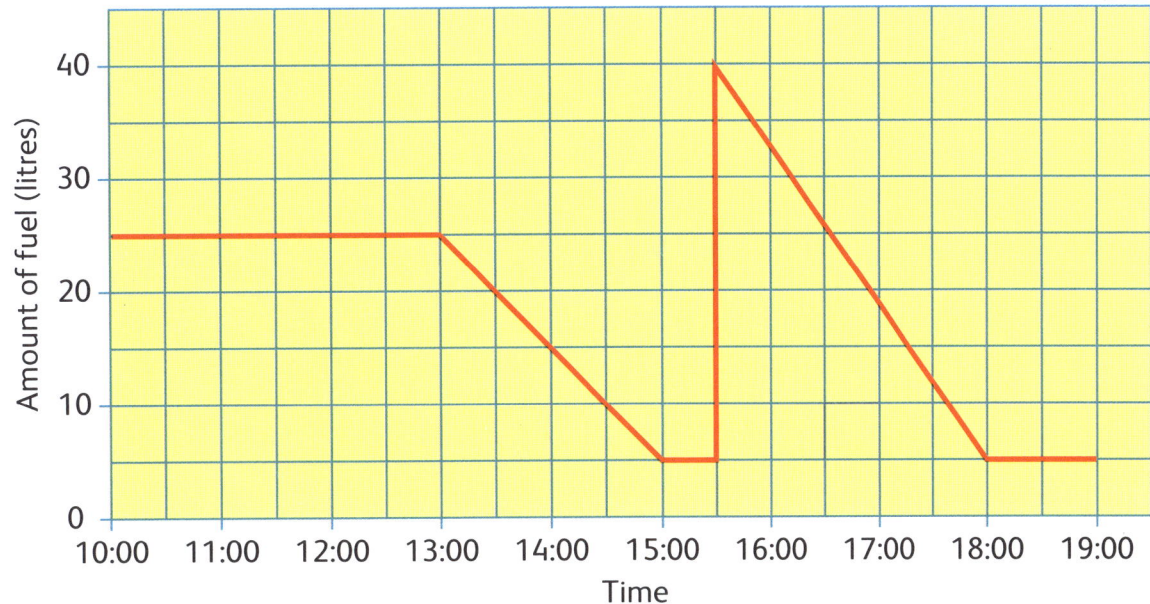

a) At what time did Stanley start his journey?

....

b) How many litres of fuel had he used before he stopped to refuel?

....

c) At what time did he fill up with fuel?

....

d) How many litres of fuel did Stanley use for his whole journey?

....

2 Bertie recorded the temperature every hour for 12 hours on the first day of his holiday. The graph shows his measurements.

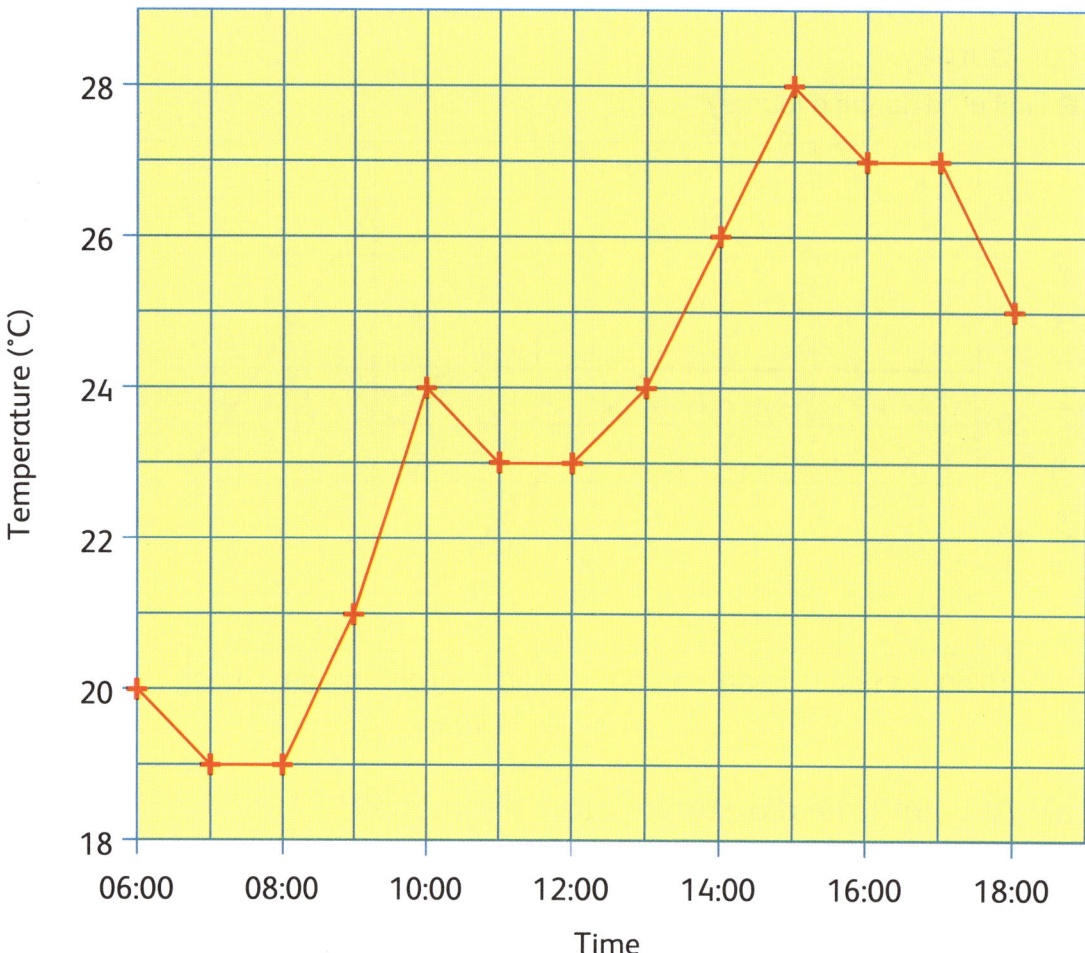

a) What was the lowest temperature he measured?
   ....

b) At what time was the temperature 28 °C?
   ....

c) What was the range of temperatures?
   ....

d) What was the mean temperature?

   ....

3 Mrs Constable recorded the temperature in her greenhouse every hour for 15 hours during one day in February. The line graph shows her results.

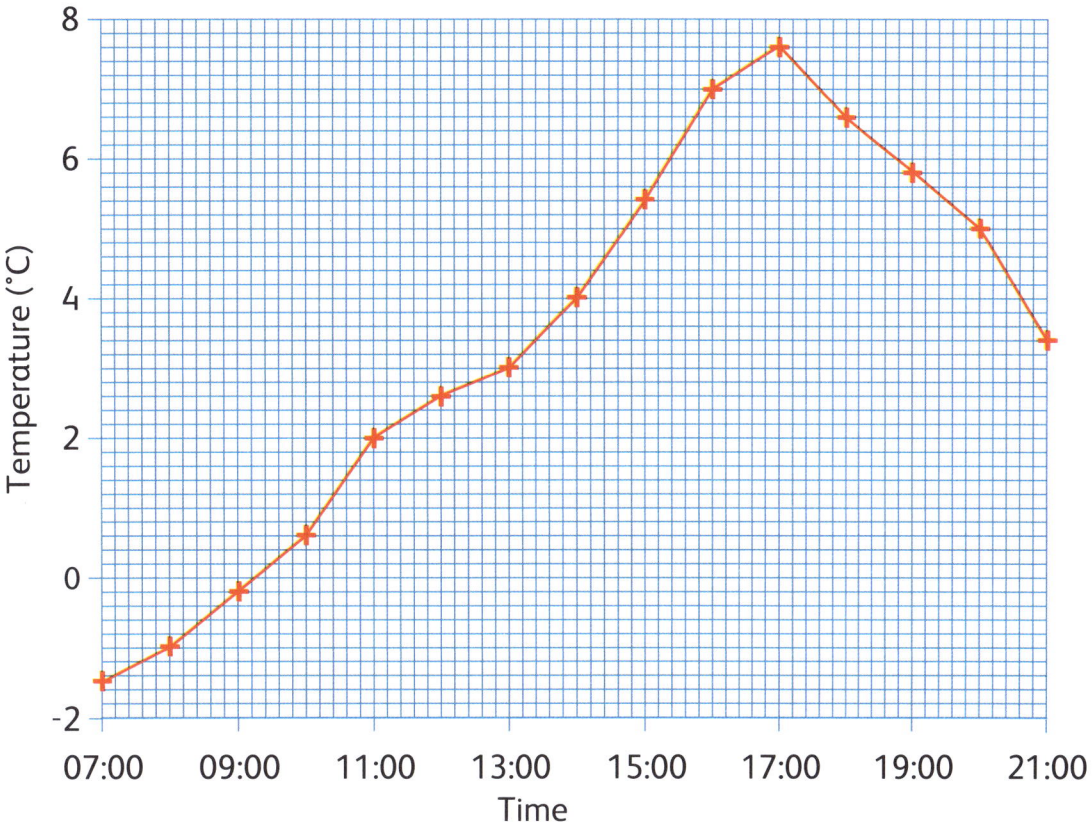

a) What was the temperature at noon?

　...

b) At what time was the lowest temperature recorded?

　...

c) What is the range of temperatures during the 15-hour period?

　...

About the practice papers

In this section, you will find four complete Ability Test practice papers. Use them as part of your preparation for your Ability Test exam.

Most of the items are similar to the ones you will see on your exam paper. This is to increase your level of comfort with the PEP exams in general. All the items will improve your reasoning and critical thinking skills.

Here are some things to remember for each practice paper:

- There are 40 items.
- You have 1 hour 15 minutes to answer all the items. This is the same time allotted for the real exam.
- Read each instruction and item carefully.
- Circle the letter of the answer you select. Under exam conditions, you will shade the letter (A, B, C, D) that corresponds to the answer you have selected for each item.
- Each item is worth 1 mark. When you, your peer or your teacher is marking the practice paper, if your answer is correct, 1 mark should be noted in the box to the right of each item. Tally your score at the end of each practice paper.

Practice paper 1

General instructions

There are 40 items in this practice paper. Read each item carefully, then circle the letter with the correct answer. There is only one correct answer for each item.

For items 1 to 3 below, select the word that best completes the statement.

1. Arm is to watch as finger is to … . ...../1

   A ring

   B gold

   C call

   D nail

2. Money is to bank as car is to … . ...../1

   A drive

   B garage

   C mud

   D highway

3. Case is to court as lesson is to … . ...../1

   A church

   B book

   C students

   D classroom

Practice paper 1

In items 4 and 5 below, which word does not belong in the group?

4 A bungalow   ..../1

   B villa

   C office

   D house

5 A soil   ..../1

   B earth

   C dirt

   D plant

For items 6 and 7 below, select the most appropriate pair of words to complete each sentence.

6 The doctor … his medical books to find a … .   ..../1

   A consult; diagnosis

   B consulted; diagnosis

   C consult; prognosis

   D consulted; prognosis

7 After hearing all the … the jury … for six hours.   ..../1

   A evidences; premeditated

   B evidences; deliberated

   C evidence; premedicated

   D evidence; deliberated

Each group below has words that are alike in some way.
Use them to answer items 8 and 9.

8 slumber   siesta   sleep   hibernate   ...../1

Which of the following is NOT like the words in the group above?

A snooze

B action

C doze

D nap

9 waste   junk   debris   scrap   ...../1

Which of the following is NOT like the words in the group above?

A litter

B rubble

C rubbish

D prized

Read the passage below carefully, then use it to answer item 10 below.

Lucy, Sarah and Amrit are the three finalists in a swimming race. Amrit takes an early lead. Sarah is not the last. Lucy does tumble turns and wears a swimming cap. Amrit touches the end wall last. Lucy comes a very close second.

10 If the above statements are true, this must mean that only one of the following statements can be true. Circle the statement you believe must be true.   ...../1

A Sarah wins the race.

B Lucy was the first swimmer to overtake Amrit.

C Amrit does not wear a swimming cap.

D Lucy wears swimming goggles as well as a swimming cap.

Practice paper 1

For items 11 to 13 below, circle the option that is an essential element of the word in bold.

11 piano
- A orchestra
- B recitals
- C keys
- D bench

...../1

12 newspaper
- A readers
- B stand
- C vendor
- D headlines

...../1

13 dictionary
- A definitions
- B language
- C pages
- D pictures

...../1

For items 14 and 15 below, select the word that comes next in the sequence.

14 majesty, majestic; trouble, troublesome; annoy, …
- A annoys
- B annoyed
- C annoying
- D annoyingly

...../1

15 tire, tiresome; judge, judgmental; help, helpful; speed, …
- A sped
- B speedy
- C speedily
- D speeding

...../1

62

Read the passage below carefully, then answer items 16 to 19.

> **A Prayer**
> *by Frank Dempster Sherman*
>
> It is my joy in life to find
>   At every turning of the road,
> The strong arm of a comrade* kind
>   To help me onward with my load.
>
> And since I have no gold to give,
>   And love alone must make amends,
> My only prayer is, while I live, –
>   God make me worthy of my friends!
>
> *comrade – close friend, brother

16 What is the main idea in the first stanza of the poem? …../1

    A The poet is annoyed that people will not leave him alone.

    B The speaker enjoys meeting people on his journeys.

    C The poet is grateful that he has friends who help him.

    D The speaker prefers carrying his burdens on his own.

17 Which line reveals how the poet truly feels about the subject of the poem? …../1

    A 'The strong arm of a comrade kind'

    B 'To help me onward with my load'

    C 'And since I have no gold to give'

    D 'God make me worthy of my friends.'

Practice paper 1

18 Here are some words translated from an artificial language. ..../1

tlezylid means sunflower

ylidzeop means flowerpot

zeopnijp means potholder

Which world could mean 'red pot'?

A tleznijp

B elsipzeop

C zeopylid

D elsipylid

19 Here are some words translated from an artificial language. ..../1

ubrenotps means bus stop

otpsgrtz means stop sign

grtzquitp means sign post

Which word could mean 'post office'?

A quitpkiptl

B quitpgrtz

C ubrenkiptl

D grtzotps

Read the passage below carefully, then use it to answer item 20 below.

> Eric, Peter, Michael, Ian and Alan play football at the weekend. They are all strikers. Peter scored nine goals more than Alan and finished between Michael and Eric. Ian did not get the lowest tally but was in single figures. Michael played every game and was top goal scorer. Eric wanted two more goals to finish joint top scorer but 17 were required.

20 If the above statements are true, this must mean that only one of the following statements can be true. Which one? Circle the statement you believe must be true.   ...../1

    A Ian scored nine goals.

    B Peter was the top scorer.

    C Ian and Alan scored the same number of goals.

    D Alan scored seven goals.

For item 21 below, select the number that completes the sequence.

21 8, 9, 16, 18, 24, 27, 32, 36, ?

    A 40   **B** 42   **C** 43   **D** 45   ...../1

Examine the pattern below. Use it to answer item 22 below.

22 Circle the answer that best completes the sequence.   ...../1

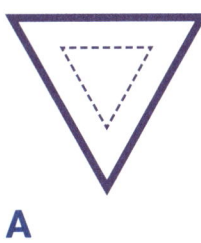  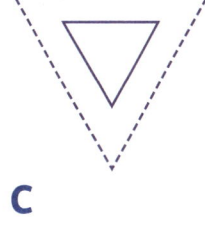 

  A   B   C   D

Practice paper 1

Look at the three groups labelled, X, Y, Z. Establish the relationship in group X. The same operation is used in group Y and group Z. Use the operation to find the missing number in group Z in item 23 below.

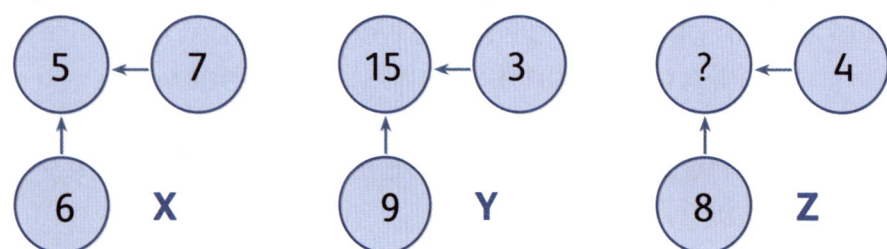

23 X (6 [5] 7)
Y (9 [15] 3)
Z (8 [?] 4)

    A 32

    B 14

    C 20

    D 12

    ....../1

24 Chairs are being set out in rows of 26 for the school play. There are 403 parents coming. How many rows of chairs are needed?

    A 16

    B 15

    C 26

    D 20

    ....../1

25 Michael is collecting football stickers. There are 640 different stickers to collect altogether. He has 452 stickers, but this includes 63 doubles (more simply he has two copies of 63 of the stickers). How many stickers is he missing?

    A 389

    B 188

    C 251

    D 577

    ....../1

26 Attendance at the Grand Gala at the National Stadium is 33,000 to the nearest 1 000. The actual attendance figure is given below. Which is it?

    A 32,244

    B 32,499

    C 33,762

    D 33,179

..../1

27 Mia has a favourite number. When she adds 4 to her number, then multiplies by 7 and finally subtracts 5, she gets 58.

What is Mia's favourite number?

    A 5

    B 6

    C 7

    D 8

..../1

28 In a group of 60 children, 24 are boys. What percentage of the group are girls?

    A 32%

    B 36%

    C 60%

    D 72%

..../1

Practice paper 1

Items 29 to 32 are concerned with the patterns below.

 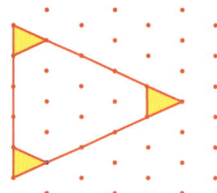 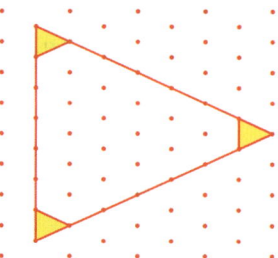

pattern 1
side length 3 units
perimeter 9 units
1 dot inside

pattern 2
side length 5 units
perimeter 15 units
6 dots inside

pattern 3
side length 7 units

29 How many shaded triangles will there be in pattern 5? ...../1

    A 6

    B 5

    C 4

    D 3

30 What is the side length of pattern 6? ...../1

    A 12

    B 13

    C 14

    D 15

31 What is the perimeter (in units) of pattern 5? ...../1

    A 33

    B 35

    C 27

    D 29

32 How many dots are there inside the white hexagon in pattern 4? ...../1

    A 28

    B 32

    C 36

    D 40

33 Colin and Lisa share 40 sweets in the ratio 3 : 5. How many more sweets does Lisa get than Colin?   ...../1

A 8

B 10

C 12

D 15

34 The table shows the proportions of different types of fruit tree in an orchard.   ...../1

Types of tree	apple	pear	plum	damson
Proportion	30%		25%	25%

There are 60 apple trees in the orchard. How many pear trees are there?

A 12

B 30

C 40

D 45

35 The pictogram below shows the results of a survey into the numbers of learners owning dogs and/or cats.   ...../1

Number of learners owning dogs	☺☺☺☺☺☺☺
Number of learners owning cats	☺☺☺☺☺☺☺☺☺

One symbol represents one learner. There are 12 learners in the class and they all own a dog or a cat or both.

How many learners own both dogs and cats?

A 0

B 2

C 3

D 4

Practice paper 1

36 Jack and Jill have buckets with capacities in the ratio 3 : 2.

They each fill identical barrels with water. Jill's barrel is full after she has made 30 trips with her bucket.

How many trips will Jack make before his barrel is full?

- A 60
- B 30
- C 20
- D 25

37 What is a half of one-third?

- A one-third
- B one-twelfth
- C one-sixth
- D two-thirds

38 A sweater normally priced at $4 500 is reduced by 20% in a sale. What is the sale price of the sweater?

- A $4 000
- B $3 600
- C $4 050
- D $3 550

39 Amy has a baking tray that can make 12 muffins at a time. Amy has an order for 100 muffins. She fills the baking tray each time before she puts it in the oven, until she has made at least 100 muffins.

How many muffins will she have left when she has delivered the order of 100?

- A 12
- B 10
- C 8
- D 6

40 The chart below represents the number of animals at Dale Farm.

Number of animals

There are six goats at Dale Farm. What is the total number of animals at Dale Farm?

...../1

A 24

B 28

C 36

D 48

Record your score ...../40

Practice paper 2

General instructions

There are 40 items in this practice paper. Read each item carefully, then circle the letter with the correct answer. There is only one correct answer for each item.

For items 1 to 3 below, select the word that best completes the statement.

1 Foot is to toe as table is to … .   …../1

    A inch

    B leg

    C chair

    D wood

2 Cake is to smear as plate is to … .   …../1

    A wash

    B serve

    C coat

    D plaque

3 Commence is to start as conclude is to … .   …../1

    A decide

    B persist

    C finish

    D commit

In items 4 and 5 below, which word does not belong in the group?

4 A football   ...../1

   B swimming

   C cricket

   D basketball

5 A capture   ...../1

   B baggage

   C container

   D suitcase

For items 6 and 7 below, select the most appropriate pair of words to complete each sentence.

6 The audience was … by the magician's stunning … .   ...../1

   A amazed; allusion

   B amused; illusion

   C amazed; illusion

   D amused; allusion

7 Homeowners are advised to … … property in case of a disaster such as fire.   ...../1

   A ensure; there

   B insure; their

   C insure; there

   D ensure; their

Practice paper 2

Each group below has words that are alike in some way.
Use them to answer items 8 and 9.

8 (grab   capture   clutch   snatch)   ...../1

Which of the following is NOT like the words in the group above?

A   take

B   seize

C   grasp

D   offer

9 (dash   rush   speed   haste)   ...../1

Which of the following is NOT like the words in the group above?

A   surge

B   urgent

C   pause

D   race

Read the passage below carefully, then use it to answer item 10 below.

Harleen, Kripa and Louise all play a musical instrument at school. Louise plays a clarinet while Harleen has to hit her instrument with a stick to make a sound. Kripa can play the piano but started with clarinet. Tuesdays are the only days that drum lessons are at school.

10 If the above statements are true, this must mean that only one   ...../1
of the following statements can be true. Circle the statement
you believe must be true.

A   Harleen has her music lesson on a Tuesday.

B   Harleen blows her instrument.

C   Louise also enjoys playing the piano.

D   Both Harleen and Louise have their lessons on the same day.

Practice paper 2

For items 11 to 13 below, circle the option that is an essential element of the word in bold.

11 essay
- A summary
- B reports
- C paragraphs
- D grammar

..../1

12 bicycle
- A wheels
- B streamers
- C helmet
- D exercise

..../1

13 church
- A pews
- B hymnals
- C organ
- D religion

..../1

For items 14 and 15 below, select the word that comes next in the sequence.

14 finance, financial; girl, girlish; laugh, laughable; create, …

- A creator
- B creative
- C creating
- D created

..../1

15 obey, obedient; elder, elderly; lady, ladylike; correct, …

- A correction
- B corrected
- C corrective
- D correcting

..../1

75

Practice paper 2

Read the passage below carefully, then answer items 16 to 19.

> Coding is one of the most productive and useful pastimes for young people to adopt. Communication skills, determination, creativity, and problem solving are just some of the immediate benefits young people can enjoy from learning to code.
>
> In addition, we live in a world that has become dependent on digital skills. Knowing how to programme will not only prepare young adults for lucrative career opportunities, but it also prepares them to navigate this digital world.

16 What does the phrase 'one of the most productive and useful pastimes for young people to adopt' suggest? ...../1

    A That young people often waste their time on meaningless activities.

    B Coding is the only worthwhile pastime for young adults because of its benefits.

    C That there are other productive and useful hobbies that young people can also enjoy.

    D Coding is an activity that only young people find useful and productive.

17 Which of the following is not a skill that young people gain from learning to code? ...../1

    A Learning to interact and share ideas with other people.

    B Sticking with a task until it is completed.

    C Using their imagination to create new ideas and things.

    D Causing disturbance for other people.

18 Why does the writer use the words, 'In addition' at the beginning of paragraph two? ...../1

    A Paragraph two is being compared with paragraph one.

    B Paragraph two solves the problem mentioned in paragraph one.

    C Paragraph two shows the results of the ideas in paragraph one.

    D Paragraph two adds to the ideas in paragraph one.

19 What do you think is the purpose of this passage? ..../1

  A To promote the benefits that young people will gain from learning to code.

  B To convince schools that they should teach learners how to code.

  C To promote the use of digital services to older people.

  D To convince older people that coding is the same thing as programming.

Read the passage below carefully, then use it to answer item 20 below.

> Ben, Mara, Lucy and Nesaar are planning their weekend together. Ben and Lucy like going to the cinema best. Mara and Nesaar enjoy bowling. Nesaar suggests ice-skating and Ben thinks it is a good idea. Mara has not been ice-skating recently.

20 If the statements above are true, this must mean that only one of the following statements can be true. Which one? Circle the statement you believe must be true. ..../1

  A Lucy prefers the cinema to bowling.

  B Nesaar does not like the cinema.

  C Ben does not like bowling.

  D Mara has more experience of bowling than ice-skating.

For item 21 below, select the number that completes the sequence.

21 6   13   27   55   111   ?

..../1

  A 225

  B 223

  C 224

  D 226

Practice paper 2

Examine the pattern below. Use it to answer item 22 below.

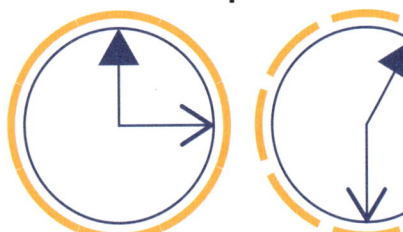 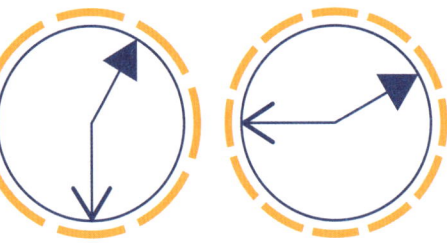 

22 Circle the answer that best completes the sequence. ..../1

   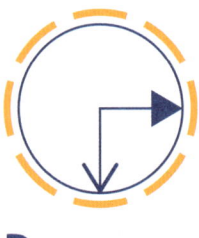

A **B** **C** **D**

Look at the three groups labelled, G, H, I. Establish the relationship in group G. The same operation is used in group H and group I. Use the operation to find the missing number in group I in item 23.

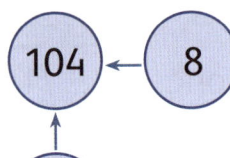 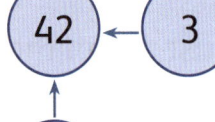 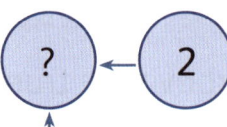

 G  H  I

23 G (13 [104] 8) ..../1
H (14 [42] 3)
I (6 [?] 2)
A 7
B 17
C 12
D 9

24 Alyssa has a favourite number. When she multiplies it by 5 and then subtracts 12, she gets her favourite number. What is Alyssa's favourite number?

A 2

B 3

C 4

D 5

25 At a rugby match, 60% of the people in the crowd are male. There are 20,000 females in the crowd. How many people are watching the match?

A 50,000

B 60,000

C 55,000

D 65,000

26 The table shows the number of goals scored by the school hockey team.

Number of goals	0	1	2	3
Number of matches	1	5	4	1

The team scored two goals in four of their matches.

What was the total number of goals scored in all of the matches?

A 16

B 17

C 14

D 15

Practice paper 2

27 Which of these routes will not take you from A to B? ..../1

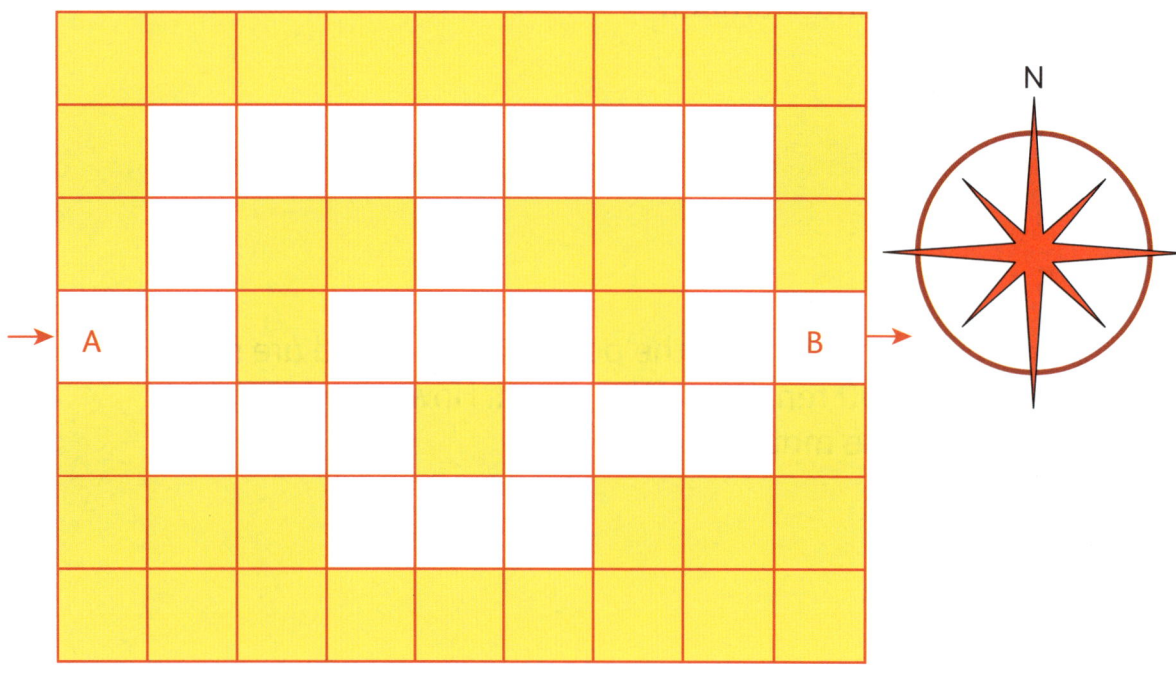

A E1–S1–E2–S1–E2–N1–E2–N1–E1

B E1–S1–E2–N1–E1–N2–E3–S2–E1

C E1–N2–E3–S2–W1–S2–E2–N1–E2–N1–E1

D E1–S1–E2–N1–E1–N2–W3–S2–W1

28 Joseph has a bag containing 20 marbles of the same size. Four marbles are blue, seven are red and the rest are green. Joseph picks a marble at random from the bag. ..../1

Which one of the following is not true?

A He is more likely to pick a green marble than a red marble.

B He has a more than even chance of picking a green marble.

C He has a one in five chance of picking a blue marble.

D He is most likely to pick a marble that is not green.

Practice paper 2

29 Here is the piece of a puzzle with area 9 cm².

Not drawn to scale

What is the perimeter of the piece?

- A 18 cm
- B 12 cm
- C 14 cm
- D 16 cm

30 Madison has two identical baking trays that can each make 12 muffins at a time. Madison has an order for 200 muffins. She fills both baking trays each time before she puts them in the oven, until she has made at least 200 muffins. How many muffins will she have left over when she has delivered the order of 200?

- A 14
- B 16
- C 12
- D 10

Practice paper 2

31 What number does the arrow indicate on the scale?   ...../1

A 2.9

B 2.85

C 2.815

D 2.83

32 In a modern dance group there are 39 boys and 26 girls.   ...../1

What fraction of the club is boys?

A $\frac{3}{5}$

B $\frac{2}{3}$

C $\frac{2}{5}$

D $\frac{3}{4}$

33 About one in every ten people is left-handed.   ...../1

Approximately how many more right-handed people than left-handed people would you expect there to be in a theatre audience of 900 people?

A 100 more

B 800 more

C 700 more

D 90 more

34 The 25 learners in a class collected data about the number of brothers and sisters they have.

.../1

Number of brothers and sisters	Number of learners
0	5
1	7
2	9
3	3
4	1

The school has a party for all 25 learners and all of their brothers and sisters. How many children will there be at the party?

A   35

B   43

C   63

D   68

35 For a school outing, the 328 learners and 32 adults are to be transported by coach. To hire a 50-seater coach costs $20,000, and to hire a 20-seater coach costs $8 000.

.../1

What is the cheapest total transport cost of taking everyone on the outing?

A $140,000

B $144,000

C $146,000

D $148,000

Practice paper 2

36 The table below shows the time Sarah spends on various activities during 24 hours.

Activity	Sleeping	Eating	Working	Relaxing	Travelling
Time (hours)	$9\frac{1}{2}$	$1\frac{3}{4}$	7		$1\frac{1}{2}$

How long does Sarah spend relaxing?

A $3\frac{3}{4}$ hours

B 4 hours

C $4\frac{1}{4}$ hours

D $4\frac{1}{2}$ hours

37 Tim walks, on average, 3 km every day.

What is the best estimate of the total distance Tim walks in a year?

A 500 km

B 1 000 km

C 1 500 km

D 2 000 km

38 The ratio of dogs to cats at a pet rescue centre is 5 : 3.

There are 18 cats at the rescue centre.

How many dogs are there?

A 20

B 25

C 30

D 45

39 Exactly five years ago, Ava was twice as old as her brother Robin.

Ava is now 11 years old.

How old is Robin now?

A 3

B 6

C 8

D 10

40 The diagram shows a maze.

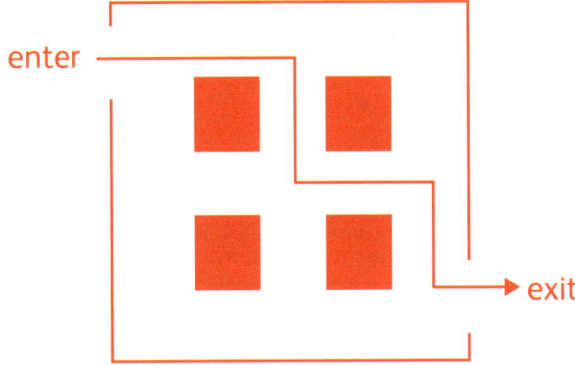

You are allowed to move in only two directions, right and down as you look at the plan.

One route through the maze is shown.

What is the total number of routes through the maze, including the one shown?

A 3

B 4

C 5

D 6

Record your score ...../40

Practice paper 3

General instructions

There are 40 items in this practice paper. Read each item carefully, then circle the letter with the correct answer. There is only one correct answer for each item.

For items 1 to 3 below, select the word that best completes the statement.

1 Give is to take as find is to … .   …../1

    A make

    B lose

    C know

    D own

2 Sail is to water as ski is to … .   …../1

    A winter

    B boot

    C snow

    D sled

3 Load is to shed as milk is to … .   …../1

    A bottle

    B spill

    C cow

    D cheese

In items 4 and 5 below, which word does not belong in the group?

4 A hexagon

   B nonagon

   C sphere

   D pentagon

5 A bottle

   B tumbler

   C glass

   D mug

For items 6 and 7 below, select the most appropriate pair of words to complete each sentence.

6 The reporter will … the public of the … trade as details become available.

   A appraise; elicit

   B apprise; elicit

   C appraise; illicit

   D apprise; illicit

7 The … has been too hot to contemplate walking … than two feet.

   A whether; farther

   B weather; farther

   C whether; further

   D weather; further

Practice paper 3

**Each group below has words that are alike in some way.
Use them to answer items 8 and 9.**

8 (decorate   adorn   brighten   renovate)   ...../1

Which of the following is NOT like the words in the group above?

A deface

B enhance

C bedeck

D garnish

9 (choose   pick   adopt   embrace)   ...../1

Which of the following is NOT like the words in the group above?

A prefer

B ignore

C favour

D select

Read the passage below carefully, then use it to answer item 10 below.

Grace, Gill, Gareth and Gavin all travel to school in different ways. Gill never walks but does take public transport. Gavin enjoys reading in the car on the way to school. Gareth has toast for breakfast. Grace cycles to school daily, unlike Gareth.

10 If the above statements are true, this must mean that only one of the following statements can be true. Circle the statement you believe must be true.

A Gavin eats cereal most mornings.

B Gareth does not cycle or take the car to school.

C Both Gavin and Gill take a train to school.

D Grace cycles past Gavin on her way to school.

For items 11 to 13 below, circle the option that is an essential element of the word in bold.

11 music
- A song
- B melody
- C listener
- D radio

....../1

12 closet
- A shelves
- B racks
- C clothes
- D drawers

....../1

13 wedding
- A couple
- B guests
- C caterer
- D planner

....../1

For items 14 and 15 below, select the word that comes next in the sequence.

14 power, powerful; month, monthly; poison, poisonous; photograph, …
- A photography
- B photographs
- C photographed
- D photographic

....../1

15 science, scientific; life, lively; damage, damaged; fool, …
- A fooled
- B foolish
- C fooling
- D foolishly

....../1

Practice paper 3

Look at the timeline below, then answer items 16 to 19.

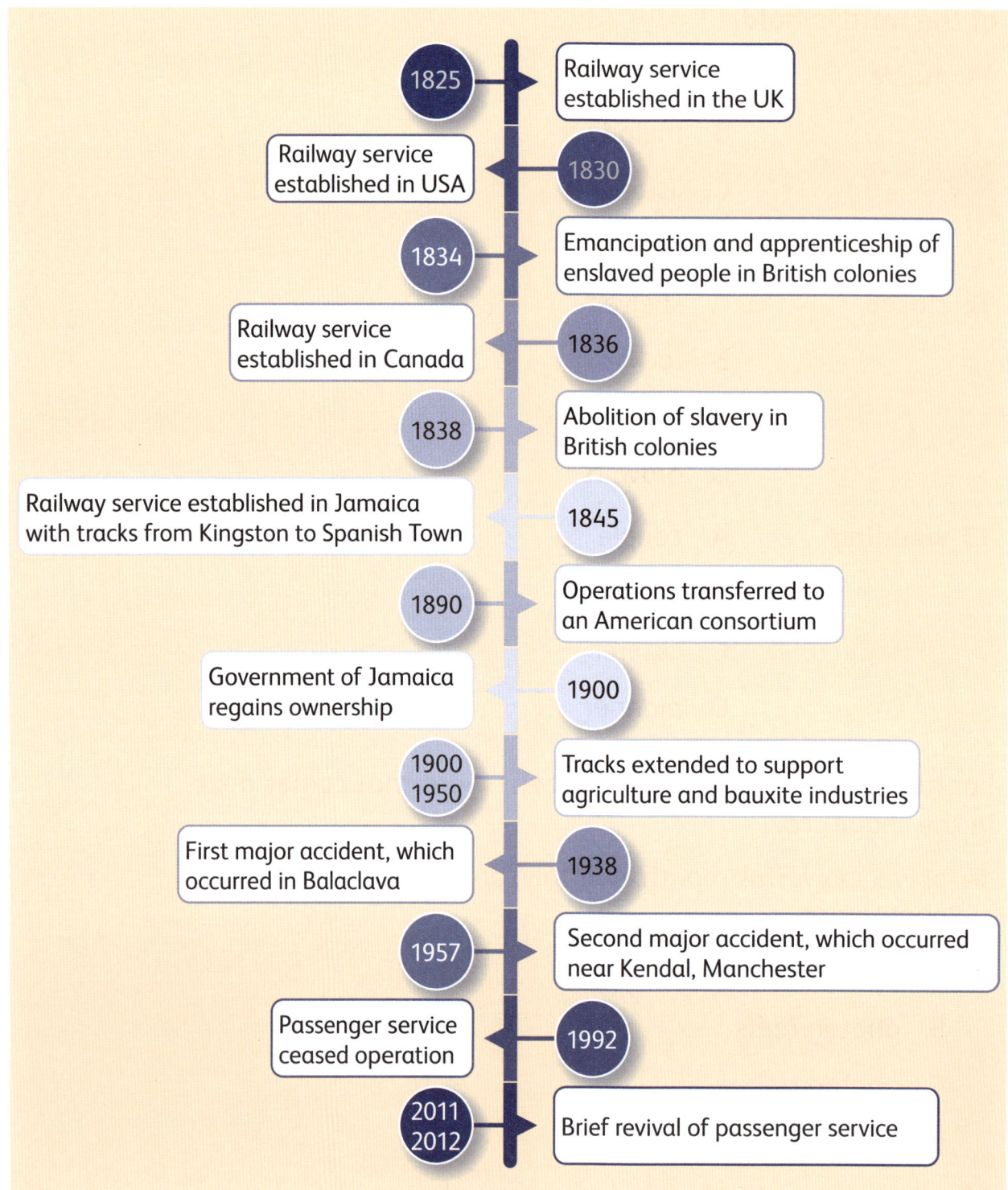

16 Why do you think the dates when railway service was established in the UK, USA and in Canada are included on this timeline? ...../1

   A to highlight how quickly railway was introduced to Jamaica after UK, USA and Canada

   B to prove that Jamaica got railway service before the rest of the world

   C to suggest that the railway service in Jamaica was better than those in the UK, USA and Canada

   D to showcase Jamaica's long association with developed countries

17 What do you think is the connection between the abolition of slavery in 1838 and the establishment of a railway service in 1945? ...../1

   A The newly freed people needed to be transported to their new jobs.

   B The railway was a sign that the newly freed people had become rich.

   C Abolition meant that slave owners needed a new way to transport their products.

   D Since slavery was abolished, there was no free labour to build the railway tracks.

18 What does an increase in the number of train tracks from 1900 to 1950 suggest about the agriculture and bauxite industries? ...../1

   A The agriculture and bauxite industries were owned by the same people.

   B They were growing and needed efficient ways to move around supplies and goods.

   C The government allowed them to use the railway free of cost to grow the economy.

   D The railway service was only used by agriculture and bauxite industries.

Practice paper 3

19 What is a good title for this timeline?

    A A history of railway service in the Commonwealth

    B The history of railway service in Jamaica

    C Railway service – then and now

    D Railway service and the Jamaican economy

Read the passage below carefully, then use it to answer item 20 below.

> Archie, Mia, Grace, Will and Molly are cousins. Mia is two years younger than Grace and one year older than Archie. Will is a year older than Mia. Molly is a year younger than Grace.

20 Which two cousins are the same age? Circle the letter.

    A Archie and Mia

    B Mia and Will

    C Will and Molly

    D Grace and Archie

For item 21 below, select the numbers that complete the sequence.

21   4   6   8   12   12   18   #   #

    A 15 and 27

    B 16 and 24

    C 14 and 20

    D 18 and 26

Examine the pattern below. Use it to answer item 22 below.

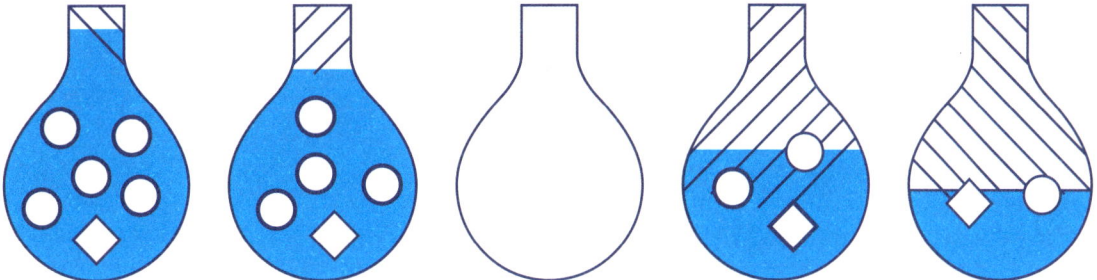

22 Circle the answer that best completes the sequence.

A　　　　　　B　　　　　　C　　　　　　D

Look at the three groups labelled, L, M, N. Establish the relationship in group L. The same operation is used in group M and group N. Use the operation to find the missing number in group N in item 23.

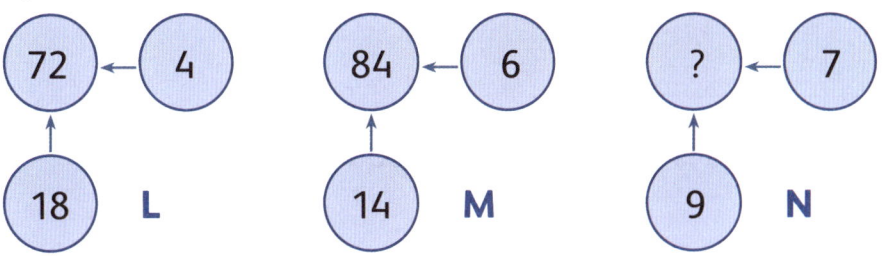

23 L (18 [72] 4)
M (14 [84] 6)
N (9 [?] 7)

　A　32
　B　30
　C　63
　D　49

Practice paper 3

24 Two apples and a mango cost $800. Three apples and a mango cost $1 060. What is the cost of a mango?

  A $260

  B $270

  C $280

  D $250

25 The diagram below shows a maze. Isaac writes his route. For example, N3 represents north three squares.

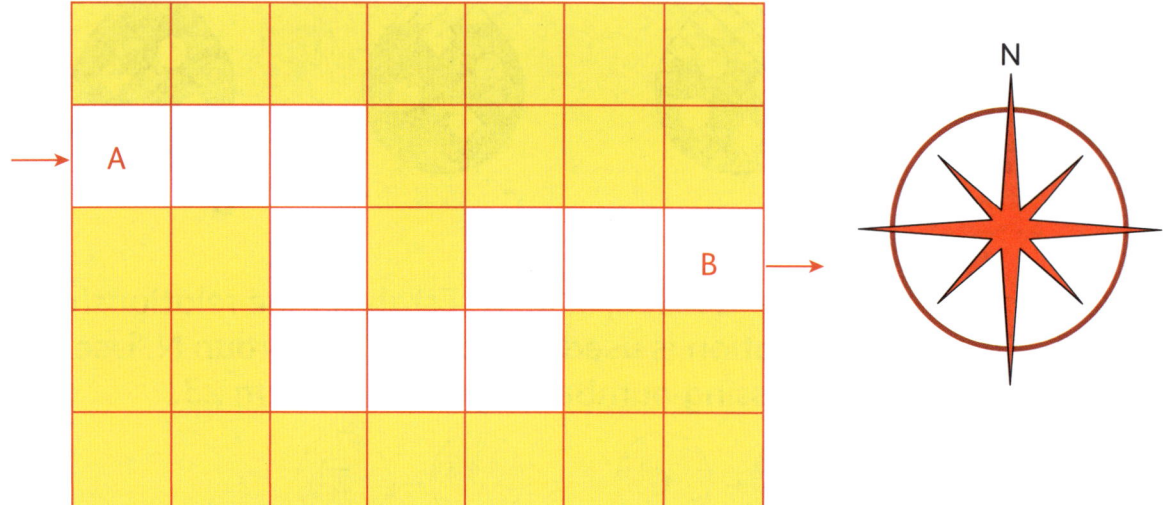

Which of the following shows Isaac's route from square A to square B?

  A W2–S2–E2–N1–E2

  B E2–S2–E2–N1–W2

  C W2–S2–E2–N1–E2

  D E2–S2–E2–N1–E2

26 In four years' time, May will be twice as old as she was two years ago. How old is May now?

  A 4

  B 6

  C 7

  D 8

27 What is the perimeter of the shape? ...../1

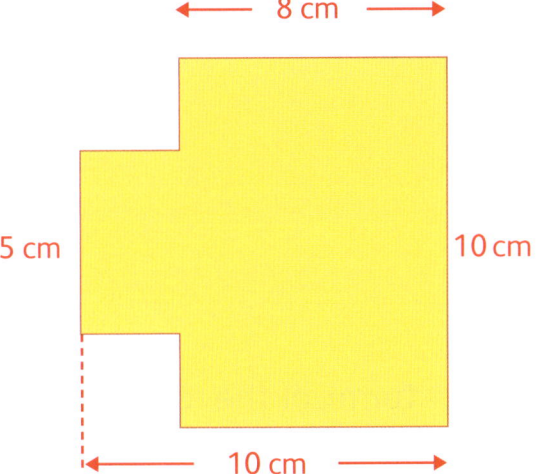

Not drawn to scale

A 36 cm

B 35 cm

C 42 cm

D 40 cm

28 The diagram shows part of a jumbled multiplication square. ...../1
Which two numbers are missing?

×	6	8	9	7
6	36	48	54	42
9	54	72		63
7	42		63	49
8	48	64	72	56

A 81, 63

B 48, 63

C 56, 81

D 54, 72

Practice paper 3

29 When the following decimals are arranged in order of increasing size, which one will be in the middle?   ...../1

3.023   3.203   2.303   2.33   3.22

  A   3.023

  B   3.203

  C   2.303

  D   2.33

30 What fraction, in its lowest terms (simplest form), of the regular hexagon is shaded?   ...../1

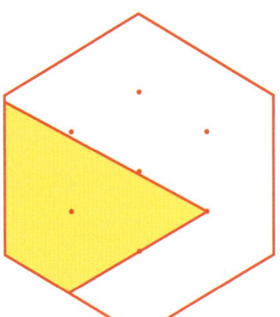

  A $\frac{1}{3}$

  B $\frac{4}{11}$

  C $\frac{5}{12}$

  D $\frac{6}{15}$

31 Charlie leaves home at 08:37 and arrives at school at 09:13. How long does it take Charlie to walk to school?   ...../1

  A   30 minutes

  B   33 minutes

  C   34 minutes

  D   36 minutes

32 How many small triangles will there be in the next pattern in this sequence? ...../1

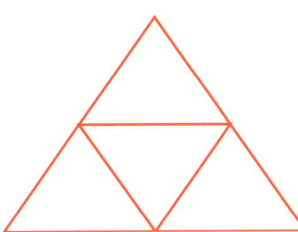
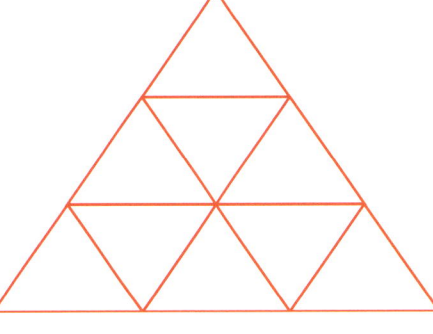

A 14   B 15   C 16   D 17

33 Bella shares her birthday cake with three friends. Amy and Bella have two slices each, Chloe has three slices and Donna has one slice. There are four slices left. ...../1

What fraction of the whole cake has Bella eaten?

A $\frac{1}{8}$

B $\frac{1}{6}$

C $\frac{1}{5}$

D $\frac{1}{4}$

34 Alice has baked a tray of muffins. ...../1

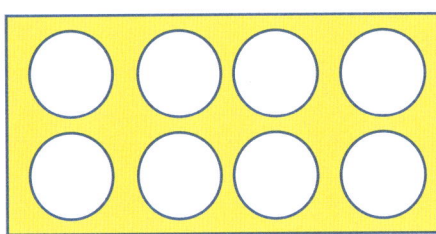

Alice eats two of the muffins.

What percentage of the muffins is left?

A 6%

B 25%

C 75%

D 80%

Practice paper 3

35 For the school outing, two buses, each capable of seating 52 people, transport the adults and children. There is one adult for every six children.

   If there are six empty seats, how many children are on the outing?

   A 84

   B 98

   C 42

   D 64

36 Gita has a set of 24 gardening books, each one with a thickness of 25 mm. She puts the books side by side on a shelf measuring 1 metre exactly.

   How much space is left on the shelf?

   A 20 cm

   B 40 cm

   C 48 cm

   D 60 cm

37 Kaylee went shopping with a $2 000 note. She bought two DVDs costing $595 each. She wrote the total cost and the change she would get from the $2 000 note.

   Which two amounts did Kaylee write?

   A $1 190, $910

   B $1 190, $810

   C $1 090, $810

   D $1 290, $810

38 The three number cards below can be placed side by side to make three-digit numbers.

For example:

3 4 5 → 3 4 5

How many different three-digit numbers, including 345, can be made using these cards?

A 3

B 4

C 5

D 6

39 Which of the following has the greatest value?

A 40% of 20

B 20% of 40

C a tenth of 80

D 8.05

40 In the wall of bricks shown below, the number on a brick is the sum of the numbers on the two bricks supporting it.

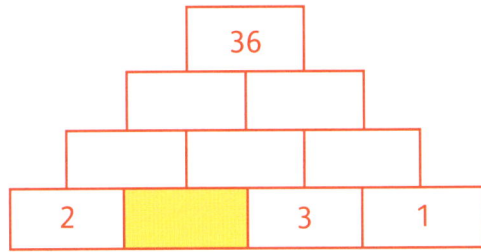

What number is on the shaded brick?

A 10

B 8

C 6

D 4

Record your score ...../40

Practice paper 4

Practice paper 4

General instructions

There are 40 items in this practice paper. Read each item carefully, then circle the letter with the correct answer. There is only one correct answer for each item.

For items 1 to 3 below, select the word that best completes the statement.

1 Broom is to sweep as cloth is to …. ...../1

    A cotton

    B mend

    C polish

    D material

2 Grow is to food as inflate is to …. ...../1

    A tyre

    B air

    C price

    D deflate

3 Ditch is to drop as retain is to …. ...../1

    A send

    B keep

    C reach

    D hole

In items 4 and 5 below, which word does not belong in the group?

4 A disguised   ...../1
    B obvious
    C clear
    D apparent

5 A ooze   ...../1
    B seep
    C leak
    D clog

For items 6 and 7 below, select the most appropriate pair of words to complete each sentence.

6 She … the entrance exam but now cannot … the offer to enrol in the programme.   ...../1
    A past: except
    B passed; except
    C passed; accept
    D past; accept

7 I will treat myself to a meal … of only … items after this exam!   ...../1
    A composed; desert
    B comprised; dessert
    C composed; dessert
    D comprised; desert

Practice paper 4

Each group below has words that are alike in some way.
Use them to answer items 8 and 9.

8 (valiant   courageous   audacious   fearless)   ..../1

Which of the following is NOT like the words in the group above?

A reticent

B brave

C heroic

D daring

9 (glower   grimace   pout   scowl)   ..../1

Which of the following is NOT like the words in the group above?

A frown

B glare

C condone

D sulk

Read the passage below carefully, then use it to answer item 10 below.

Adam, Gauri, Aryan and Zephan all attend the same dance club. Adam and Gauri love tap classes but do not do street. Zephan adores disco whereas his friend Aryan detests modern; his favourite is salsa. All the children do salsa dancing but only Gauri prefers waltz.

10 If the above statements are true, this must mean that only one of the following statements can be true. Which one? Circle the statement you believe must be true.

A Gauri attends three types of dance classes.

B Zephan does not enjoy disco.

C They all dance on a Friday.

D Adam likes three types of dance.

For items 11 to 13 below, circle the option that is an essential element of the word in **bold**.

11 cinema
- A movie
- B snacks
- C intermission
- D advertisements

..../1

12 palace
- A staff
- B guards
- C royalty
- D dungeon

..../1

13 parable
- A dilemma
- B characters
- C plot
- D lesson

..../1

For items 14 and 15 below, select the word that comes next in the sequence.

14 improve, improved; chill, chilly; enjoy, enjoyable; forget, …

- A forgetful
- B forgotten
- C forgot
- D forgetfully

..../1

15 shake, shakeable; wind, windy; hate, hateful; continue, …

- A continuously
- B continuous
- C continued
- D continuing

..../1

Practice paper 4

Read the passage below carefully, then answer items 16 to 19.

> All children, except one, grow up. They soon know that they will grow up, and the way Wendy knew was this. One day when she was two years old, she was playing in a garden, and she plucked another flower and ran with it to her mother. I suppose she must have looked rather delightful, for Mrs. Darling put her hand to her heart and cried, "Oh, why can't you remain like this for ever!" This was all that passed between them on the subject, but henceforth Wendy knew that she must grow up. You always know after you are two. Two is the beginning of the end.
>
> *Extract from Peter Pan by J M Barrie*

16 Why is the phrase 'except one' used in the first sentence? ...../1

  A To introduce an air of mystery

  B To suggest that the main character dies before growing up

  C To introduce the readers to Wendy

  D To suggest that Mrs Darling is a child at heart

17 Which of the following is a synonym for the word 'delightful' as used in the passage? ...../1

  A boring

  B enchanting

  C disturbing

  D frustrating

18 Why did Mrs Darling put her hand on her heart as she said, "Oh, why can't you remain like this for ever!"? ...../1

  A She was hiding her disapproval of Wendy plucking her flower.

  B She was regretting that Wendy would grow up and lose her innocence.

  C She was eager for Wendy to grow up and be more ladylike.

  D She was aware that Wendy was the child that would not grow up.

19 Why was two such a significant age for Wendy?

   A She stopped playing in the garden.

   B Her relationship with her mother changed.

   C Her mother revealed she was the child that would not grow up.

   D She became aware that growing up meant change.

Read the passage below carefully, then use it to answer item 20 below.

> Eddy, Casper, Amy and Eve are comparing the homework they need to do today. Eddy and Eve both have maths homework. Casper is finishing a geography project tonight. Amy and Eddy both have history homework. Casper often leaves his homework until the last minute.

20 If the statements above are true, this must mean that only one of the following statements can be true. Which one? Circle the statement you believe must be true.

   A Casper's geography project is due tomorrow.

   B Amy is never given maths homework.

   C Eddy has at least two pieces of homework to complete.

   D Amy does not like geography.

For item 21 below, select the numbers that complete the sequence.

21

24, 30, 37, 45, 54, *, *

   A 65 and 76

   B 63 and 77

   C 69 and 79

   D 64 and 75

Practice paper 4

Examine the pattern below. Use it to answer item 22 below.

22 Circle the answer that best completes the sequence. ..../1

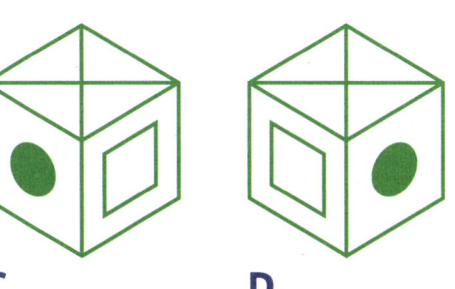

A   B   C   D

Look at the three groups labelled R, S, T. Establish the relationship in group R. The same operation is used in group S and group T. Use the operation to find the missing number in group T in item 23.

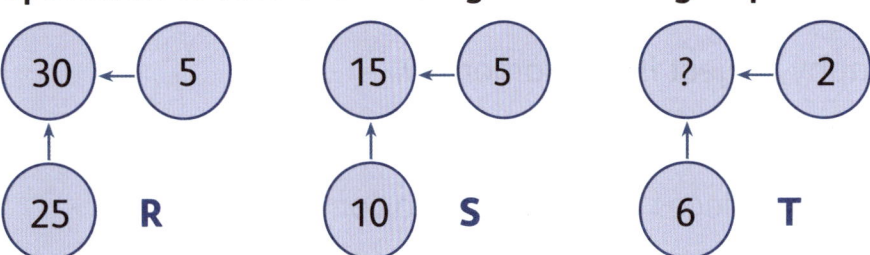

23 R (25 [30] 5) ..../1
S (10 [15] 5)
T (6 [?] 2)

  A 8

  B 16

  C 6

  D 0

24 Violet is thinking of a number, *v*. Rose is thinking of a number that is 7 less than Violet's number. Which expression shows Rose's number, *r*?

   A $r = v + 7$

   B $r = v - 7$

   C $v = r - 7$

   D $v = r + 7$

Items 25 and 26 are concerned with the table of data prepared by six friends.

Name	Age (Y:M)	Mass (kg)	Height (m)	Eye colour
Alice	10:7	45	1.48	blue
Ben	10:6	39	1.37	brown
Clare	10:9	40	1.54	blue
David	11:0	41	1.49	green
Emily	10:5	38	1.62	blue
Flora	10:8	44	1.47	brown

25 Who is 2 kg heavier than Ben?

   A Alice

   B Ben

   C Clare

   D David

26 Which friend with blue eyes is older than Flora?

   A Alice

   B Ben

   C Clare

   D David

Practice paper 4

27 Aisha bakes five dozen muffins to be sold at a fair. She sells two-thirds of the muffins at $50 each and then reduces the price by 10% for the remaining muffins and sells all of them.

How much money does she make?

..../1

- A $2 900
- B $2 800
- C $2 600
- D $3 200

28 A rectangle with side lengths of whole centimetres has area 36 cm². Which of the following could not be the perimeter of the rectangle?

..../1

- A 30 cm
- B 40 cm
- C 74 cm
- D 28 cm

29 In a card game, a cat scores the same as three dogs and a dog scores 3 less than a cow. The four cards in Crystal's hand score a total of 15 points.

..../1

Which of the following groups of four cards could Crystal have?

- A cow, cow, cow, cat
- B dog, dog, dog, dog
- C cat, dog, dog, cow
- D cat, dog, cow, cow

30 James' walking pace distance is 90 cm and Jenny's walking pace distance is 80 cm. They set off together and walk the distance between two trees. James walks 72 paces.

How many more, or fewer, paces does Jenny walk than James?

A 10 fewer

B 10 more

C 9 fewer

D 9 more

..../1

31 A coffee costs c dollars and a muffin costs m dollars. A group of four friends have a coffee and muffin each and then two of them have a second coffee and one of them has a second muffin.

What is the total cost, in dollars, of the coffees and muffins?

A $4c + 5m$

B $5c + 4m$

C $6c + 4m$

D $6c + 5m$

..../1

32 The perimeter of the shaded square is 12 cm.

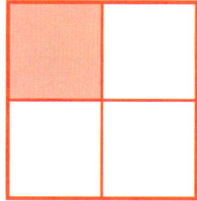

What is the area of the large square?

A 36 cm²

B 24 cm²

C 48 cm²

D 64 cm²

..../1

33 $a - 2b = 5c$

Which of the following is correct?

A $a + 5c = 2b$

B $5c + 2b = a$

C $2a - 4b = 5c$

D $2b - a = 5c$

34 The table shows the proportions of different types of tree in a wood.

Types of tree	ash	beech	chestnut	oak
Proportion	28%	14%		44%

There are 56 ash trees in the wood.

How many chestnut trees are there?

A 14

B 24

C 32

D 56

35 Which of the following gives a different result from all of the others?

A a third of 21

B $4 \times 1\frac{1}{2}$

C 30×0.2

D $1 + 2 \times 2$

36 Andy, Barbara and Clare start with 20 marbles each. ...../1

In the first round, Andy wins five marbles from Barbara, Barbara loses seven marbles to Clare, and Clare wins six from Andy.

In the second round, Andy loses 14 marbles to Barbara, Barbara wins eight from Clare and Clare loses four to Andy.

Which of the following represents the numbers of marbles each player has at the end of round two?

A A9, B30, C21

B A11, B22, C27

C A16, B17, C27

D A11, B33, C16

37 Which of the following is the largest? ...../1

A 4%

B $\frac{4}{5}$

C 0.405

D 42%

38 The picture shows a bag of vegetables on a balance. ...../1

The needle shows the mass in kilograms. What would be the reading on the balance if 500 g of vegetables were removed from the sack?

A 0.9 kg

B 1.9 kg

C 1.7 kg

D 0.8 kg

Practice paper 4

39 The sum of the masses of the 24 children in a class is 1320 kg. ..../1
What is the average mass of a child?

    A 55 kg

    B 48 kg

    C 45 kg

    D 56 kg

40 This diagram is used to sort shapes.

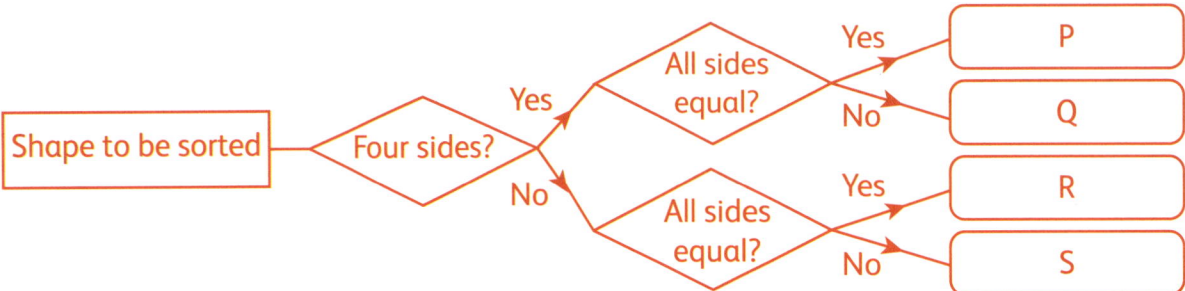

Which of the following pairs of shapes would be sorted into box Q? ..../1

    A rhombus, kite

    B square, rhombus

    C scalene triangle, parallelogram

    D rectangle, trapezium

Record your score ..../40

Exam tips and guidelines

Here are some tips and guidelines in case you feel anxious and overwhelmed as you get closer to the day of your exam.

In the months leading up to your exam:

- Build your critical thinking skills in all subject areas. What you learn in the other subjects will help you to understand the test items on the Ability Test paper. You will also be able to link ideas and use logical reasoning to find the correct answers.
- Ask your teacher to go over the steps for the item styles that you don't quite understand. You can also read through the steps in this volume and complete the worksheets.
- Pace yourself. Understand one item style before you move on to the next.
- Attempt the first practice paper, when you feel confident.
- Look at the items that you did not score a mark for, then review the notes and steps for those item styles. Attempt to answer the same items a second time. If you still are not able to find the correct answer, ask your teacher for help.

One week before the exam:

- Revise the item styles and work through the practice papers in both Volume 1 and Volume 2.
- Explain to a classmate who does not understand an item style.
- Practise!

The day before the exam:

- Make sure you are well rested. Try to relax the afternoon before your exam and get a good night's sleep.
- Be around people who have a positive attitude.
- Prepare your exam kit with pencils, pens, erasers and whatever else you are allowed to take with you to the exam.
- Do not try any new foods.

Exam tips and guidelines

The day of the exam:
- Eat your usual breakfast.
- Make sure you have your exam kit.
- Get to the exam location early so that you are relaxed and comfortable.
- Do your best!

Feeling anxious and overwhelmed before an exam is perfectly normal. Take a deep breath and remember that you have been preparing for it for months, so just do your best.